D1218092

WORD OF GOD, WORD OF EARTH

WORD OF GOD, WORD OF EARTH

DAVIE NAPIER

A PILGRIM PRESS BOOK
FROM
UNITED CHURCH PRESS

Library of Congress Cataloging in Publication Data

Napier, Bunyan Davie.
    Word of God, word of earth.

    "A Pilgrim Press book."
    Includes the author's edited translation of selected passages from the Old Testament book of 1st Kings.
    1. Elijah, the prophet—Addresses, essays, lectures.
    2. Bible. O. T. 1 Kings XVII-XIX, XXI—Criticism, interpretation, etc.—Addresses, essays, lectures.
    3. Pastoral theology—Addresses, essays, lectures.
    I. Bible. O. T. 1 Kings XVII-XIX, XXI. English. Napier. 1976. II. Title.
    BS580.E4N36   222'.53'077   75-45312
    ISBN 0-8298-0304-1
    ISBN 0-8298-0307-6 pbk.

Excerpts from The Jerusalem Bible (JB) are copyright © 1966 by Darton, Longman & Todd, Ltd. and Doubleday & Company, Inc. Used by permission of the publisher. Biblical quotations from The New English Bible (NEB) are © The Delegates of the Oxford University Press and the Syndics of the Cambridge University Press 1961, 1970. Reprinted by permission. Scriptural excerpts from The New American Bible (NAB) are © 1970 and used herein by permission of the Confraternity of Christian Doctrine, copyright owner. Quotations from the Revised Standard Version Bible (RSV) are copyright 1946, 1952 and © 1971 by the Division of Christian Education, National Council of Churches and are used by permission. The excerpts on pages 70 and 76 from Letters to a Young Poet by Rainer Maria Rilke, translated by M. D. Herter Norton are reprinted by permission of W. W. Norton & Company, Inc. Copyright 1934 by W. W. Norton & Company, Inc. Copyright renewed 1962 by M. D. Herter Norton. Revised Edition Copyright 1954 by W. W. Norton & Company, Inc.

United Church Press, 1505 Race Street, Philadelphia, Pennsylvania   19102

CONTENTS

PREFACE   12

I THE DROUGHT: 1 KINGS 17   18

    THE CRISIS   20

    HEALING: THE WORD AND ACT OF THE PROPHET   22

    KERITH: VV. 2-7   27

    FLOUR AND OIL: VV. 8-16   28

    SICKNESS UNTO DEATH: VV. 17-24   30

II THE ALTARS: 1 KINGS 18   36

    THE CONTINUING CRISIS   39

    THREE PERSONS: VV. 2b-19   41

      Ahab and Obadiah: vv. 2b-6   41

      Obadiah and Elijah: vv. 7-15   42

      Elijah and Ahab: vv. 16-19   43

    TWO ALTARS: VV. 20-40   45

    ONE PRIEST: VV. 41-46   50

III THE CAVE: 1 KINGS 19   54

    ON THE WAY TO THE CAVE: VV. 2-6a, 8   58

    THE STAY AT THE CAVE: VV. 9a, 11b, 12-15a, 18   61

    THE WAY BACK FROM THE CAVE: VV. 19-21   68

IV THE INHERITANCE: 1 KINGS 21   74

    A RILKE WORD   76

    WORD OF GOD, WORD OF EARTH   76

    ON ADJACENCY   79

    BY VIOLATION AND VIOLENCE   82

    IN THE NAME OF GOD   83

    THE QUESTION AND THE QUESTIONS   86

APPENDIX: A STUDY GUIDE   90

NOTES   96

ABOUT THE AUTHOR   105

PREFACE

These essays came into being in response to the invitation of the Yale Divinity School to deliver the 1975 Lyman Beecher Lectures. They have to do with ministry and the minister, with the task and the person of anyone pledged by whatever process and committed under whatever kind of covenant to biblical faith and biblical values. They deal with ministry, lay as well as professional, in response to Word of God and word of earth.

The model for these studies is the prophet Elijah, or, we might better say, the texts about him in 1 Kings, and the composer or composers of his stories. What do we see and say of ministry now, in the last quarter of the twentieth century, as suggested out of events occurring in fact or in saga in the ninth century before our era, long before the Bible dreamed to be, nine centuries before the time of Jesus and Paul, three hundred years in advance of the Second Isaiah and a full century before the First?

Elijah is the earliest viable biblical model for ministry. The figure of Moses, at least three centuries earlier, is much more shaped out of the stuff of a people's long-sustained corporate historical reflection. Samuel, in the century preceding Elijah's, comes down to us blurred and self-contradictory in the union of conflicting traditions. And of the contrast between Elijah in the ninth and two other prophets of the preceding tenth century, the late Prof. Gerhard von Rad commented, "The pictures drawn in the Old Testament of Nathan or Ahijah of Shiloh may seem curiously lifeless: but in the stories about Elijah we are suddenly confronted with a clearly drawn historical figure."[1] The fact is, of course, that classical Old Testament prophetism really begins with Elijah.[2]

I have lived for a longer time and more intimately with Elijah than with any others of the prophets. My doctoral dissertation was a detailed analysis of the Elijah texts and of the related Elisha material. Ninth-century (B.C.E.) Israel has remained an epoch of particular fascination for me. It has been good to pick it up again, explore it again, and again to confront (and be confronted by) that phenomenal figure, the first of the classical prophets.

My own preparation for these essays/lectures began with a fresh, critical reading and translation of the Hebrew texts of 1 Kings 17-19, 21, and I have reproduced, as preface to each of the chapters, the results of my work as editor and translator. As I shall have to say again, such dramatic stories as these have inevitably drawn additions, accretions, from subsequent traditionists. These edited translations are simply one modern reader's effort, in consultation with the works of scholars of this century, to achieve a reading more closely approximating what may well have been the Elijah material as it took form in the years during and immediately following his own time.

My very particular thanks to Deans Colin Williams and Harry Adams of the Yale Divinity School; to (they will know why) the ministers of the Rocky Mountain Conference of the United Church of Christ; to Prof. Millar Burrows; and to Joy.

Abbreviations:

JB   *The Jerusalem Bible* (Garden City, N.Y.: Doubleday, 1966).
NAB   *The New American Bible* (New York: Kenedy, 1970).
NEB   *The New English Bible* (Oxford, 1970).
RSV   *The Revised Standard Version* (New York: Nelson, 1952).

WORD OF GOD, WORD OF EARTH

I
THE DROUGHT:
1 KINGS 17

1 Elijah the Tishbite said to Ahab, "By the life of Yahweh the God of Israel whom I serve, I declare that in these immediate years there shall be neither dew nor rain but at my word." **2,3** Then the Word of Yahweh instructed him: "Get out of here and **4** keep heading east; hide in the Wadi Kerith at the Jordan. You will be able to drink from the stream; and I have commanded the ravens to feed you there." So he put into action the Word of **5** Yahweh: he went to live in the ravine of Kerith where it **6** approaches the Jordan; and the ravens kept bringing him food, and he drank from the stream.

7 But after a while, of course, the stream petered out because **8** there had been no rain on the earth. So the Word of Yahweh **9** advised him again: "Move immediately to Zarephath, a Sidonian town, and take up your residence there. You will see: I've designated a local woman, a widow, to sustain you."

10 Accordingly, he picked up and went to Zarephath, where, coming into the town, he saw in fact a woman, a widow, gathering sticks. So he called to her and said, "Will you bring me, please, something with a little water in it, so that I can **11** drink." And as she started out to get it, he called out after her, **12** "Will you also bring me please a piece of bread." But now she responded, "I swear by the life of Yahweh your God, there is nothing baked left, but only a handful of flour in a jar and a little oil in a cruet. You just found me gathering a few sticks to **13** prepare this for my son and me to eat before we die." Elijah said to her, "Don't be afraid. Go ahead with what you propose to do; but in addition and first make out of it a small biscuit for me, and bring it to me. You may then take care of yourself and **14** your son; because this is the Word of Yahweh the God of Israel:

> The jar of flour shall not be finished
> And the cruet of oil shall remain undiminished
> 'Til the time when Yahweh again has replenished
> The face of the ground with rain."

15 She carried out the word of Elijah; and she was sustained, she, **16** and he, and her son, day after day. The jar of flour was not consumed, nor the cruet of oil depleted, in accord with the Word of Yahweh which was declared through Elijah.

17 Some time after all of this, it happened that the son of this woman, who was mistress of her own house, was taken ill; and his condition became so severe that he was hardly able to

18 breathe. Now she spoke to Elijah: "Why did you interfere, you man of God? You've come to me to expose my own sin, and so

19 to kill my son." "Give me your son," he said; and taking him from her arms he carried him to the upper room [Elijah's own

20 room] and put him down on the bed. Then he cried out, aloud, to Yahweh: "Yahweh, my God, can it be your intention, in addition [to the drought and attendant disasters], to inflict catastrophe on the very widow who has opened her home to

21a me by killing her son?" Then he stretched himself out on the

22b, 23 child three times with the result that he revived. Elijah picked up the child, brought him down from the upper room of the house, and giving him back to his mother, he said, "See, your

24 son lives." The woman responded, "Now I know in fact that you are a man of God, and that the Word of Yahweh that you speak [literally, in your mouth] is truth."

THE CRISIS

In significant and irreversible ways these years of the final quarter of this century seem more than mere decades removed from the fifties and early sixties. The pace of change, if not always its effect, has been revolutionary.

I received a powerful dose of revolutionary-paced change in a single academic year when, in the fall of 1966, we moved to Stanford University from a teaching position in Yale Divinity School and residence in the Master's House of Calhoun College. The ways of Yale College have, to be sure, changed drastically since then; but in the year of our departure, we were still enforcing the coat-and-tie rule in the college dining halls. In loco parentis still prevailed. Following college dances we were supposed, at least, to be sure that women guests (the college was of course still all-male) were no longer lingering in student rooms. We were baptized into Stanford University, by contrast, in the year of David Harris' student-body presidency, into an academic environment that had been coeducational from the beginning and that was in process of "coeducating" all student housing. Not only was there no coat-and-tie rule; there was not even a shoe rule. The consequent experience of revolutionary change gave me the worst case of the cultural bends I have ever had.

Perhaps especially for those of us who are responsibly related to the theological enterprise and the church, the years since the fifties have drastically altered us in sensitivity, in conscience, in perception. Names of persons, places, and events of these years having particular impact on me, and even so by no means exhaustive, may be suggestive of how and why and in what degree we have been moved from where we were: Frantz Fanon, Malcolm X, Eldridge Cleaver, Stokely Carmichael, Rap Brown, Martin Luther King, Jr., James Cone; Seoul, Saigon, Santiago; meetings of church people at places like Bangkok and Medellin; and church people like Philip Potter and Claire Randall; and voices, writers, and prophets like Ivan Illich, Gary MacEoin, Paulo Freire, Gustavo Gutierrez, Rosemary Ruether, Rubem Alves, Dom Helder Camara, José Miranda; and colleagues like John Bennett and Robert McAfee Brown; and events like Berkeley in 1964, and in subsequent years Stanford and Vietnam and Columbia and Vietnam and Harvard and Vietnam, and Vietnam and Cambodia; and Yale and Mayday; and Jackson State and Kent State; and Watergate; and still Vietnam. Two worlds of the cold war have become three worlds, with the anguish and poverty and oppression of the third interpenetrating the two and declaring to all of us in our world that things will never be the same again. And with all this there is the certain knowledge among us that the years of plenty of this planet's resources are really already ended and that we must learn to live, if we will live at all, in relative drought.

Elijah's word to Ahab must now be the declaration of a permanent if not terminal condition. The years, the centuries, the millennia of ample dew and rain of resources and of their profligate exploitation are over. The fecundity of the earth, which the Ahabs and Jezebels have always worshiped and appropriated, has been bled to barrenness. Neither Elijah's word nor even Yahweh's will restore it. This drought will endure. Of this kind of dew and rain, there shall be no more.

I do not see how contemporary ministry, particularly on the ancient prophetic model, can be faithful either to the Word of God or the word of earth except as it is lived and preached in a sense of critical, responsible, passionate urgency. And both these words—of God and of earth—must be heard and proclaimed simultaneously. Rubém Alves, Latin American theologian and church person, claims the support of the likes of a Karl Barth on the one hand and a Paul Lehmann on the other when he says that "the language of the community of faith must be understood as occurring between the reading of the Bible and the reading of newspapers."[1]

Or, as a contemporary French theologian has put it, "If the Church wishes to deal with the real questions of the modern world [then] instead of using only revelation and tradition as starting points . . . it must start with facts and questions derived from history."[2]

The Word of God and the word of earth—earth as nature, as history, as humanity. That beautiful and sensitive prophet of earth U Thant said in 1969 that the member states of the United Nations have a decade to solve the major problems of the world before "they have reached such staggering proportions that they will be beyond our capacity to control."[3] Another earth prophet, Evelyn Hutchinson, looking not at the political but the ecological aspects of crisis, gives us a little more time:

Many people . . . are concluding on the basis of mounting and reasonable objective evidence that the length of life on the biosphere as an inhabitable region for organisms is to be measured in decades rather than in hundreds of millions of years. This is entirely the fault of our own species.[4]

Those prophets of earth who gave us that sobering if not alarming study called *The Limits to Growth* see that ultimate point reached within a century, if present trends continue in population, pollution, industrialization, food production, and resource depletion. The result will be sudden and uncontrollable decline. The factors that will undo us proceed, by and large, along lines of exponential not simple linear escalation. Our situation may be compared to that of the owner of a pond on which a lily grows in the middle, doubling in size each day so as to cover the pond and choke off all other life in it in thirty days. The owner says, "It's OK. I won't worry about it until the pond is half covered." And when is that? On the twenty-ninth day.[5]

It is the biblical creation faith that we are charged with the responsible care of the earth. It is the Word of God that demands our hearing and responding to the word of earth. The authentic voices of earth tell us who minister that our ministry is set in crisis: Neither nature nor history, neither history nor humanity, can longer survive, without heretofore unimaginable consequences, the sustained ruthless exploitation inflicted upon them by the powerful of the earth. The authors of *The Limits to Growth*, prophets of earth, are speaking more than ecologically when they suggest quietly that it is still possible to alter trends and to produce a global equilibrium designed "so that the basic material needs of each person on earth are satisfied and [everyone has] an equal opportunity to realize [one's] individual human potential."[6]

HEALING: THE WORD AND ACT OF THE PROPHET

Elijah to Ahab; prophet to king; minister to constituency; church to its own members and to this world: In the years that are coming upon us there shall be neither dew nor rain. Conditions and terms of existence which have obtained until now and upon which we have been accustomed to rely will obtain no more. Drought, the crisis of alienated folk in an alienated earth, calls for radical response; and it is the sense of the text that any satisfactory resolution of crisis will result from the prophetic word, the word and act of ministry. There shall be neither dew nor rain except at my word. The only solution lies beyond the destruction of Baal, amoral symbol of unlimited potency.

Of course this is to take liberties with the model, as is only appropriate. At the end of the next chapter, 1 Kings 18, Elijah effects the termination of the same drought which he proclaims in the story before us. But the living biblical word is not delivered to us in the hard rigidity of rigor mortis. It comes to us moving and alive. In the Elijah story, the life-sustaining resources recur by the action and word of ministry—when Baal has been effectively destroyed, when the gods and goddesses of fecund, unlimited productivity are repudiated, when personal and tribal gratification are disaffirmed and Yahweh is acclaimed ultimate, whose will it is always to bring Israel out of Egypt, Philistia out of Caphtor, Syria out of Kir; to whom Judah and Ethiopia are alike; who calls for highways between the Egypts and the Assyrias of the earth; who blesses all human families, calling them all my people, the work of my hands, my heritage.[7]

If we are to take these texts as suggesting authentic qualities of contemporary ministry, then we may be startled here, if not even a little disconcerted, by the measure of authority, bordering on arrogance, assumed to obtain to the prophet. There shall be neither dew nor rain except at my word, unless and until I say so. We remember that Mosaic tradition holds Moses culpable for arrogating to himself and Aaron power to produce water in the sustained drought of the wilderness. Before striking the rock from which fresh water is to gush forth, Moses cries, in long-pent-up exasperation, "Listen to me, you rebels. Must we get water out of this rock for you?" It is the harsh judgment of tradition that this indiscretion was responsible for his failure to enter the promised land.[8] Our conventional piety, then, might lead us to expect another reading in the Elijah story: "There shall be neither dew nor rain except at the Word of Yahweh." We've grown accustomed to the phrase—and very comfortable with it—that God is working in history. The real worker in the Elijah stories, as for the most part in the narratives of subsequent prophets, is the prophet himself; and with uncommon emphasis in the Elijah texts, the word and the act of his ministry are seen as authoritative, efficacious, and decisive—derivative, of course, of the Word of Yahweh.

It is nevertheless a matter which has obviously disturbed the traditionists, who have on occasion taken it upon themselves to "improve" the narratives according to their own taste. Elijah comes on too strong for them. In the statement that the prophet and the widow and her son were all sustained, the qualifying phrase that this was according to the word of Elijah is omitted by some Greek translators centuries later as being in improper conflict with the Word of Yahweh (in vv. 5 and 16). Even some English translators eschew the phrase "the word of Elijah" and render it "she did as Elijah had said" or "had told her."

But if we take seriously this model for ministry, it may be reprimanding us for our timidity, our failure to speak and act incisively and with authority, our fear to declare the word of earth in the name of God, our disposition to say that only God can speak and act to redeem the catastrophic conditions of our human drought, the now apparently impending disaster of our exploitation of earth and humanity. If we impute any sense of revelation to these narratives, any authentic disclosure of the meaning of ministry, then the word and act of our ministry must run the risk even of appearing brash. The function of ministry must be effective response to the word of earth—to be sure, in the name of God, but with the understanding that its implementation is up to us. If it is done, we will do it, to be sure in response to the Word of God and the Holy Spirit.

At a recent commencement at Pacific School of Religion, our seniors asked John Fry to give the commencement sermon. He is on the faculty of our sister seminary at San Anselmo, a former Chicago pastor distinguished then and now for a total work of ministry sensitive and responsive to the word of earth, the raucous, anguished, bitter, revolutionary word of the cheated of the earth. The piety of some in our constituency was offended not only by his vehement insistence that if the work of ministry to earth is done, it is ours to do—God will not himself do it—but that we must think and hear and act on our own initiative and on our own determination of the nature and urgency of the Word of God and of earth. This is what he said, in part:

> Here's what I'm proposing. . . . I propose, first, that you forget about assistance from the side of the universe at large, that is, from Exalted Justice, some tendency, in Being as such, for fair play and righteousness. It's not there. A corollary of this proposal is that any exalting of justice is going to have to come from you. The Bible can't go to Delano tomorrow with food, clothes, and money for farm workers. The Bible is going to stay on its shelf right over there in that chapel. People can go, carrying all the food and money I'm sure you've given. Maybe you'll go along. But here's the point: If Chavez finally loses, don't go making up theological explanations about the promise of God. You take the rap. It'll be your rap to take.
>
> I propose second: When you walk out of here today, you really walk out on your own, and stay on your own from now on. A part of the infantilizing procedures in theological education, which

I've already noted, consists of hearing the truth from Daddy who heard it from some other bigger person who heard it from Augustine who heard it from Paul who heard it from God. Well, what do you think? Ask that question, and here's what one gets: a twenty-page paper on what all the big people think. But you, in your incomparable subjectivity, and all that native intelligence, with those great GRE's and a splendid Rorschach; yes, you, right there; what do you think? Was Arius right or Nicaea right? Quick, now; don't go to the library. Don't look up your lecture notes. On your own tell us—what do you think? It may look like the old authority question, but it's not. It's the old Peter Pan question about staying children always, even though M.Div. and even Ph.D. Lo, I tell you a mystery. I've known religious figures sixty years old who, when they die, could have chiseled on their tombstones these immortal words: "Niebuhr says, Barth says, Brunner says, but Tillich says." And these figures, what do they say? One doesn't know. They've never said. They will have gone from birth to death without thinking one single thought absolutely and lustily on their own. You want that? Ruether says, Pannenberg says, Cone says, Loomer says—well, that's the dismal prospect, unless you feel desperate and decide to make the move pretty quick, unless you get up out of here, on your own. And were you to have participated in the exaggerated traditions of the past, at one point in the ceremony you all would have switched your tassels from the right to the left. And that's what I might have urged you to do—to swing that tassel from the right to the left with objective force, really move it over there, and keep on going the same way.

My last proposal, and end of the speech, is: Pinch yourself to make sure you're not dreaming this whole thing, this beautiful day, in this gorgeous setting. You are never going to be in a place like this again: all your papers finished, in the company of so many people who know you so well and love you so much. From now on, it's broken glass, and shotguns, and live rattlesnakes, and children dying for a drink of water in sub-Sahara Africa, and policemen who sneer when they say "Reverend." So soak it up. You didn't earn it, so it must be grace. Enjoy it! It may be a long, long time before it comes again. Let's have a lot of crying and hugging and kissing and dancing and carrying on around here after the serious is over—something to remember in the trying days up ahead when, like the wild asses I hope to God you'll be, you go out there and get some justice![9]

These words are in affinity with the sense of the Elijah model: Ministry is the *work* of justice, and ministry must hear and hold and speak its own word, its own independent word, formed and advised to be sure by the cross of the horizontal and the vertical, at the intersection of the Bible and the newspaper, in the meeting of the word of earth and the Word of God.

Some of our number who professed offense at Fry's failure to commend the ready availability of the power of God were no doubt even more disturbed by his hearty admonition that they follow their tassels resolutely to the left. Most of us, knowing John Fry and acknowledging the whole context of the occasion, were willing to impute to his word of earth the presence of the Word of God.[10]

But in any case, there can be no ambivalence on this point in our texts. The *first* word of Elijah that we hear is a declaration of the essence of ministry, its foundation, its inspiration, its compulsion, its sense, its reason for being: As Yahweh the God of Israel lives . . . by the very life of Yahweh God of Israel . . . before whom I stand . . . whom I serve . . . in whose presence I live and move and have my being . . . in the name, for the sake, to the glory, toward the will, and at the call and command of Yahweh, God, Embodiment of Justice, ultimate Mother and Father of all the living, patient lover of oppressed and oppressor—by this life, which is the only Way and Truth I know, I speak what I must speak, and do what I must do!

There is always talk of the loss of the vertical in the life of the church to an alleged increasing preoccupation with horizontal concerns. But how can the Word of God and the word of earth be held separate? Prophetic ministry knows neither, alone, and is able to understand the one only in immediate consciousness of the other. If one says to Elijah that he should leave matters of the drought to engineers and rainmakers, famine and poverty to the appropriate bureaucracies, human healing to the AMA, foreign affairs to Samaria/Washington, the scandals of Baal worship to the self-policing of the multinational corporations, the murderous appropriation of the little vineyards of the little Naboths around the world to the justice and the greed of the powerful, and the peace of the world to Ahab's chariots and the Pentagon—Elijah will have to say, and we in the church will have to say, We cannot do this without denying that Yahweh lives; or without removing ourselves from his presence.

Three scenes follow in 1 Kings 17, all during and in consequence of the drought. In the first, Elijah survives worsening drought and famine in the Wadi Kerith. In the second he takes up what proves to be sustaining residence with a Sidonian widow. And in the third he restores to life and health her dying son. Since all three strain the credulity of our very proper, precise, scientific, square mentality, let us suspend *that* inhibiting quality of mind; or, better, let us begin to abandon altogether the solid, Western, whitish, malish, prudent, reasoned stance, in which we appear to have become frozen, and, for the permanent conditions of crisis ahead of us, let us like Elijah learn to rest lightly on the earth. This means that we will say of nothing (shades of Screwtape), This is mine; that we will regard no condition as established; that we will remain in every sense mobile; and that we will cultivate, embrace, and affirm the graces of speedy improvisation. If we are to minister now in response to Word of God and word of earth, we must be (in frame of mind if not in reality) without place, without possession, without people, without position; and insofar as we use them, we must know that they are not ours. To attempt to hold them is, if not immediately to perish, to die to ministry. In this indefinite—I think permanent—term of crisis of the earth, the fixed base, professional, geographical, theological, ideological, with its assumption of permanence is surely ultimately an illusion.

KERITH: VV. 2-7

Our posture in the world reminds me of lines I've had stuck in my mind since early childhood:

The boy stood on the burning deck
  Eating peanuts by the peck.
His father called; he would not go
  Because he loved the peanuts so.

Elijah leaves the place he's been. We really don't *know* where he came from, or even where he is when he turns eastward to be sustained by the hospitality of ravens and the diminishing flow of a brook. We meet Elijah first wherever Ahab is, and it is apparently the assumption of the narrative that everyone knows where the king is. The formal fortress/palace, built by Ahab's father, Omri, is on the summit of Samaria; but it is probable that the primary home and residence of both kings is Jezreel.[11]

The word either of God or of earth or both may tell us—Elijah is an authentic model—to go for the sake of the survival and preservation of our ministry where, if we eat at all, it will be (what an act of trust!) at the beak of ravens. It is amusing to see what rationalists among modern commentators have proposed as alternate readings for "ravens," since that is of course a patent absurdity. By changing the vowels (which were not in fact a part of the original Hebrew text), we can read "Arabs." Or, others have argued, a case can be made, without change in the word, to "merchants." Or, according to another proposal, since the root underlying "ravens" carries the meaning "to be black," why don't we assume that Elijah was fed by Blacks? The rationalization is hardly better than the inference of miracle, predicating as it does Arabs or merchants or Blacks coming in daily parade through the wadi, this rough, wild, godforsaken ravine, to share with Elijah the contents of their brown paper bags. Blacks feeding a White? Arabs feeding a Jew? Merchants feeding a prophet? "Ravens" is better.

An interesting aside: The Spanish Bible translates "ravens" as *los cuervos,* one meaning of which, in addition to black birds, is "corrupt priests." Let the commentators play around with that one.

The model calls us to the recovery of a lost virtue, if indeed we ever owned it. Ministry is to Word and earth, and we have made of it an institution, a profession. We in ordained ministry are quick to condemn our professional colleagues in medicine or law or even teaching for the abandonment of the motive of service for that of compensation. We are the ones who ought to know that the deck is burning; but our love of peanuts is not always demonstrably less than theirs. It is a cultural assumption to which we have become totally accommodated that the only reason one moves anywhere from Samaria or Jezreel is because it is a move "up" in pay and prestige.

Two or three years after we had left Stanford, we returned to attend a farewell party for a Medical School professor and his family we had come to know well. At table, someone spoke with regret of our having left Stanford and expressed the supposition that, even if we had wanted to stay, we could not have afforded to turn down the offer of a seminary presidency. My wife replied casually, "No, we took a cut." Now I break in to say that the deck is hot, but that I too am very fond of peanuts and have more than my share in spite of that cut. Later in the evening, the same friend put her arm around Joy and said comfortingly and sympathetically, "I hope Davie's next move will be up."

FLOUR AND OIL: VV. 8-16

In the second scene of the chapter, the circumstances for prophetic ministerial survival and promotion are hardly improved. The resources of amiable ravens and dying stream are to be replaced by the dubious, tenuous hospitality of an absolutely unknown and unidentified woman, a widow, and she far to the north, quite beyond the borders of Israel-Judah, in a town of Sidon through and on the other side of Queen Jezebel's home territory of Tyre. Elijah must have said, Yahweh, you've gotta be kidding!

Now we won't torture the model. Not everything fits. Where it speaks, let it speak. Where, being only itself, it cannot be also for us, then let it be, and be comfortable letting it be. Or take it for itself alone. Elijah comes through, if not always as a winsome guy, as fully and on the whole admirable *person*, prophet, minister. He has enormous strengths, together with the whole range of qualities of unimpeachable, authentic humanity. And he and his story are blessed with an original narrator (or narrators) of equal distinction in his own calling. Despite some insensitive, overly pious, and marring accretions, we are aware that the story of Elijah is economically, simply, and brilliantly told.

There is of course absurdity in every act of faith. To live in faith in the time of our own perilous drought is to live in the assumption that if there is no bread, ravens will bring us bread; or that the widow's exhausted and nonrenewable ingredients for the preservation of life—the testimony of the word of earth—may by the Word of God *and our own bold word and ministry* be made sufficient for the whole household.

Jesus welcomed the crowds [in the thousands] and spoke to them of the kingdom of God, and cured those who had need of healing. Now the day began to wear away . . . [and he said to his disciples], "You give them something to eat." They said, "All we have is five loaves and two fish. . . ." "Make the people sit down in groups of fifty or so," Jesus said. Then, taking the five loaves and the two fish, he looked up to heaven, and blessed and broke them, and gave them to the disciples to set before the crowd. And all ate and were satisfied.[12]

The widow said to Elijah [obviously in outrage and indignation], "I swear by the life of Yahweh your God, there is nothing baked left, but only a handful of flour in a jar and a little oil in a cruet. . . ." [But] she carried out the word of Elijah; and she was sustained, she and he, and her son, day after day. The jar of flour was not consumed, nor the cruet of oil depleted, in accord with the Word of Yahweh which was declared through Elijah.

The Word of God and the word of earth:

It is still possible to alter trends and to produce a global equilibrium designed "so that the basic material needs of each person on earth are satisfied and that all persons have an equal opportunity to realize their individual human potential."[13]

I've said, Don't torture the model. Don't make rigid the process of correspondence between Elijah's ninth B.C.E. and our twentieth A.D. The symbol of drought is effective and appropriate and authentic in our times—we know this; it doesn't have to be said—in ways quite beyond, but surely related to, the ecological crisis. Forms of our drought include, of course, institutionalized racism, institutionalized violence, institutionalized hypocrisy/arrogance/greed; institutionalized-nationalized-USized imperialism; institutionalized devices and procedures in operation around the world to grind the faces of the poor in the dirt and keep them there; and, by these same devices and procedures, to assure the continued flow of wealth and the desirable goods of the world into the pockets and mouths and establishments of those who already control and possess in grotesque disproportion the produce and products of the earth.

SICKNESS UNTO DEATH: VV. 17-24

This time of drought is also a time of sickness unto death. If the monumental pious declarations and postures of our past were ever justified, it cannot be now or ever again. To talk piously, superficially, glibly, and with detachment, as too often we have, of the unfolding drama of the Bible; of God who acts; of the redemption of history in God's good time; of the inevitability of the perennial presence of the poor among us, of war among us; to do so in such a way as to denigrate or disparage or depreciate the word and work and anguish of earth, the epidemic hunger and poverty and impotence that afflict like the plague most of the human family—to thus stalk across the earth in these impervious boots of a monarchical Word of God is to castrate the prophets and lobotomize Jesus Christ. We cannot now, if we ever could, afford this kind of piety, which doesn't even say, Let George do it. It says, Let God do it! Nor can we, in the midst of this vast human drought which has overtaken us, presume always to be polite to God (to say nothing of each other) and therefore to be deceiving, dissimulating. On the authority of what ancient, outmoded model do we stand only in awe before the presence of the Presence—in abject confession, in (often) self-concerned petition, in (sometimes essentially) self-seeking intercession, or in cheap, insubstantial (and it may be, illogical) thanksgiving? This is the God who wills power to the people, all God's people, all people, and not to kings and emperors and other assorted oppressors. This is the God of the poor, the oppressed, the abused, the exploited, not the god of the mighty. In James Cone's symbolic use of the terms, this is the God of the Blacks, not the god of the Whites. God knows us. We can't get by with pretension in that Presence. So, along with prayers of Thanksgiving and Confession and Intercession and Petition, let's let fly with the prayer of Protest. There is splendid precedent, authoritative example.

Here is Moses:

Why do you treat your servant so badly? ... Why are you so displeased with me that you burden me with all this people? Was it I who conceived all this people? or was it I who gave them birth, that you tell me to carry them at my bosom, like a foster father carrying an infant, to the land you have promised under oath to their fathers? Where can I get meat to give to all this people? For they are crying to me, "Give us meat for our food." I cannot carry all this people by myself, for they are too heavy for me. If this is the way you will deal with me, then please do me the favor of killing me at once, so that I need no longer face this distress.[14]

There is Job, of course, in that bitter parody of Psalm 8:

Why do you rear man at all,
Or pay any mind to him?
Inspect him every morning,
Test him every moment?
Will you never look away from me?
Leave me be till I swallow my spittle?[15]

Put a little differently: What are people, men and women, that you make so much of them, that you set your mind on them, visiting them every morning and testing them every moment? Will you never look away from me or leave me alone long enough for me to swallow my spit?

And Jeremiah (rendering all the lines as address to Yahweh in a prayer of Protest):

> Yahweh, you have deceived me, and I was deceived;
> You are stronger than I, and you have prevailed.
> I have become a laughingstock all the day; everyone mocks me.
> For whenever I speak, I cry out, I shout, "Violence and Destruction!"
> For your Word has become for me a reproach and derision all day long.
> If I say, "I will not mention you, or speak anymore in your name,"
> There is in my heart as it were a burning fire shut up in my bones,
> And I am weary with holding it in, and I cannot.[16]

And Habakkuk, like Jeremiah coming very close to home:

> How long, Yahweh, am I to cry for help
> while you will not listen;
> to cry "Oppression!" in your ear
> and you will not save?
>
> Why do you set injustice before me,
> why do you look on where there is tyranny?
> Outrage and violence, this is all I see,
> all is contention, and discord flourishes.
>
> And so the law loses its hold,
> and justice never shows itself.
> Yes, the wicked man gets the better of the upright,
> and so justice is seen to be distorted.[17]

And so back to Elijah and his own brief, incredulous prayer, charged with resentment and outrage if, as he fears, the little son of the widow is dead. A properly pious prayer has been added to the text, in an effort to preserve in Elijah the conventional image of the man of God; but the true and authentic word of the narrative is this: In profound exasperation and anguish of spirit, with the seemingly lifeless body of the child now lying on the prophet's own bed, Elijah cries in unmistakable meaning, Are you really going to go through with this? As if privation of earth and people were not already enough, can you bring totally undeserved judgment on this child and on his mother by taking his life, leaving her now in consummate grief, and me in contempt and rejection? My God Yahweh!

The child, whether dead or not, lives. Renewed life or healing, or both, has occurred. We do not even have to bend the model: The lay and professional minister, ministry, is acutely vulnerable to the word of earth, the human condition, as it confronts the life of ministry; and because ministry knows that the Word of God is the Word of Yahweh, God of Israel, God of the Servant, God of the Gospel, it understands that it must play its own role, speak its own word, fulfill its own function, affirm its own identity and integrity, and act its own part in responding to the Word of God and the word of earth.

Giving the child back to his mother, Elijah said, "See, your son lives." She responded, "Now I know in fact that you are a man of God, and that the word of Yahweh that you speak is truth."

The model is vastly simpler than our reality. But it is clear in its directive that the life of our earth is threatened as never before and that the progeny of the family of which we are a part are in critical and immediate need of healing. We have not come yet to the end of our story. The child is before us. We are called to heal, to run the risk of failing as well as the risk of succeeding. We must speak and act, toward the earth with sensitivity and compassion and courage, toward God and each other without pretense, and toward ourselves with initiative, integrity, and boldness, sensitive to the Word of God and vulnerable to the word of earth.

II
THE ALTARS:
1 KINGS 18

1   After a long while, this Word of Yahweh occurred to Elijah:
     You can go now to face Ahab; I'm ready to let it rain over the
2   land. So Elijah went to confront Ahab.

3   Since the famine was critical in Samaria, Ahab called in
     Obadiah, his chief steward [omitting 3b-4 with many schol-
5   ars] and said to him, "Come on; we'll explore all the sources of
     water and all the wadis in the land in hopes of finding enough
     grass to save at least some of our horses and mules and so not
6   lose all our animals." Then dividing the land between them for
     their search, Ahab went one way, and Obadiah took the other
     way by himself.

7   Now, while Obadiah was on his way, whom should he encoun-
     ter but Elijah; and recognizing him, he fell on his face. Then he
8   said, "So it is really you, my Lord Elijah?" He answered, "It is!
9   Go say to your master, 'I've just seen Elijah!'" But Obadiah
     countered, "What have you got against me, that you consign
10   this servant of yours to death at Ahab's hand? By the life of
     Yahweh your God, the nation or kingdom doesn't exist to
     which my master hasn't already sent to apprehend you; and
     when they answered, 'He isn't here,' he demanded a formal
     declaration from that kingdom or nation that you were not to
11   be found. And you're telling me to go say to my master, 'I've
12   just seen Elijah!' What will happen? As soon as I leave you, the
     Spirit of Yahweh will whisk you away I know not where; I
     will go in to report to Ahab; and when he can't find you, he will
     kill me—and I, your servant, I've been from childhood on a
13   Yahweh worshiper! Has no one told you, my Lord, what I did
     when Jezebel slaughtered the prophets of Yahweh; that I hid a
     hundred of the Yahweh prophets in caves, by fifties, and kept
14   them supplied with food and drink? And now you command
     me to announce to my master that Elijah is here! He will kill
15   me!" Elijah replied, "I swear by the life of Yahweh of hosts
     whom I serve [to whom I am committed or in whose presence I
     live] that I will confront him this very day."

16   Obadiah then left to intercept Ahab; and when he broke the
17   news to him, Ahab went to meet Elijah. As soon as Ahab saw
     Elijah, Ahab said to him, "Is it [really] you, you troubler of
18   Israel?" Elijah answered, "I'm not the one who's troubled
19a Israel, but you and your father's entourage. Now will you
     convene all Israel for me at Mount Carmel [with support

20 omitting all 19b]." So Ahab sent a summons throughout Israel
21 and brought all of the people together on Mount Carmel. Elijah
        stood and addressed them all: "How long will you go on
        vacillating between the two alternatives? If Yahweh is God,
        follow him; or if Baal, follow him." The people answered him
22 not a word. Again Elijah addressed the people: "I myself am
        the only prophet of Yahweh left; but the prophets of Baal
23a number four hundred fifty. Now let us have two bulls [23a]."
25a Then to the prophets of Baal, Elijah said, "You all choose one
        of the bulls and prepare it first, because there are a lot of you
23c, 24 [25a]; and I will myself prepare the other bull [23c]. You pray
        aloud in the name of your God as I will do in the name of
        Yahweh; and it shall be that the God who responds with fire,
        he is God." To which all the people responded with a shout of
        approval [24].

26 Accordingly, they [the prophets of Baal] took the bull, pre-
        pared the sacrifice, and from morning until noon they prayed
        in the name of Baal, shouting, "O Baal, answer us!" But there
27 was no sound, nor any response. Now they performed their
        limping dance around the altar they had made; until at noon
        Elijah called out, taunting them, "Cry louder, for he is a god:
        maybe he's meditating; or he's gone to the john; or he's off on a
28 trip; or perhaps he's asleep and needs to be waked up." Crying
        louder and louder, and in conformity with their tradition, they
        gashed themselves with swords and spears until they were
29 bleeding profusely. Even with the passing of midday, they
        continued in prophetic ecstasy; but there was no voice, there
30 was no answer, there was no sign of attention. Then Elijah
        said to all the people, "Come in closer toward me"; and they all
        moved in toward him. He rebuilt the [old] Yahweh altar which
33 was in ruins [omitting 31-32], laid the wood [for the fire],
        carved the bull and placed it on the wood. Then he said
37 [omitting to v. 37], "Answer me, Yahweh, answer me, so that
        this people may know that you, Yahweh, are God, and that as
        you let them go from you, it is yours also to bring them back."[1]
        Then the fire of Yahweh struck [omitting the balance of v. 38],
39 and when the people saw it, they fell, prone, and then cried,
40 "Yahweh, he is God; Yahweh, he is God!"[2] Elijah said to the
        people, "Seize the prophets of Baal; let none of them escape."
        They seized them; and Elijah led them down to the Wadi
        Kishon and slaughtered them there.[3]

41 Now Elijah said to Ahab, "Get moving; eat and drink; because
42 there is the sound of the swish of rain." So Ahab went to eat
    and drink; but as for Elijah, he climbed up to the top of Carmel
    and crouched down on the ground with his face between his
43 knees. He said to his servant, "Go over there, now; look out to
    sea." He went and looked: "'There is nothing at all," he said.
44 Seven times Elijah asked him to go back; and in fact the
    seventh time, he reported, "Yes—I can see a cloud no bigger
    than a man's hand rising up out of the sea." Elijah said, "Go tell
    Ahab, 'Harness your chariot and get going, before the rain
45 stops you.'" Even as this was taking place, the skies grew dark
    with clouds, the wind came, and then heavy rain. Ahab
46 mounted his chariot and made for Jezreel; and with [as it were]
    the hand of Yahweh upon him, Elijah pulled himself together[4]
    and went, as runner to the chariot, all the way to Jezreel.

THE CONTINUING CRISIS

The fundamental and perennial circumstance of crisis has always obtained for a majority of the people of earth, although many of them, as now, living tenuously, perilously, miserably, vulnerably, have been innocent of a sense of crisis. If in all ages some have believed themselves to be, or have in fact been, on relatively secure and durable plateaus; if, as appears to be the case, some of our present companions of earth regard the conditions of their life as being thus established and unassailable, such an assessment is now patently naïve. The crisis of the relatively secure of the earth is made the more critical by their real, or it may well be feigned, complacency. One wonders whether apparently confident, comfortable, successful church persons are, in the depth of their being, as certain of the durability and righteous justification of their status of relative vast privilege in the world as appearances are contrived to suggest. Is the sociologist-critic of the church describing the real thing or a masquerade of both people and preacher when he writes, "It is as if there had been no Sermon on the Mount. . . . Sunday will remain the same: the American silent majority sitting righteously in the pews listening to silent sermons."[5] Pretended complacency, if that is what it is, is profoundly sick and makes the condition of crisis the more insidious.

But it is much more than this, isn't it? We, the privileged of earth, have appropriated and exploited the earth and all that is in it, the world and those who dwell therein; we have founded our folly now even upon the seas; and we have established the ineradicable marks of our vandalism over the virginal, variegated, speechless faces of the earth and, by the billion, on the innocent and until now largely submissive faces of the human family. Jacques-Yves Cousteau, explorer, lover and physician of the oceans, has written of the fabulous, creative, life-sustaining qualities of the seas:

> Surely this blessed miracle of life is the greatest treasure on earth. Yet do we humans cherish and guard it? On the contrary. Each month we now pour so many millions of tons of poisonous waste into the living sea that in perhaps twenty years, perhaps sooner, the oceans will have received their mortal wound and will start to die.[6]

Who is we? All of us together of the earth are pushing in number close to four billion. But we who have our way in the earth are only about 30 percent of the total, living in North America, Europe, the

Soviet Union, and Japan. We earn generally more than $3,000 a year, which is well over $8 a day. We consume 92 percent of the world's energy (the United States alone takes a third), and most of the other mineral wealth of the earth. The other 70 percent of the world's population get by on an average 65 cents a day and divide among themselves the remaining 8 percent of the world's energy and its leftover minerals.[7]

And this too, of course, heightens and intensifies the very critical tensions of our time with which, for an indefinite future, we shall have to live. From among our own oppressed in North America and Europe, as well as from the Third World continents of Latin America, Asia, and Africa, eloquent voices, many from our own ranks of church and ministry, are telling us, the 30 percent, that these conditions of gross inequity and imbalance may not and will not endure. Innocence of the ghastly conditions of their particular human crisis—grinding poverty, economic slavery, disease; malnutrition that stunts the development of the brain and maims intelligence; thwarted, inhibited stature, physical and psychological; shockingly premature death—innocence of this awful truth is at a furious pace giving way to a new consciousness and conscience, to conscientization. The day of the sustained maintenance of the conditions of the comfortable, secure, developed plateau are over.

> The poor countries [writes the Peruvian priest, Father Gustavo Gutierrez] are becoming ever more clearly aware that their under development is only the by-product of the development of other countries. . . . Moreover, they are realizing that their own development will come about only with a struggle to break the domination of the rich countries. . . . A broad and deep aspiration for liberation inflames the history of mankind in our day, liberation from all that limits or keeps man from self-fulfillment, liberation from all impediments to the exercise of his freedom.[8]

Part of the definition of our own condition of crisis—crisis USA— lies precisely here. If we say to Father Gutierrez, "Power to your revolution; power to your people," he will respond, as he has, that "there can be authentic development for Latin America only if there is liberation from the domination exercised by the great capitalist countries, and especially by the most powerful, the United States of America."[9]

It is most emphatically not my intention to suggest solutions for these overwhelming problems of earth out of the ancient narratives about Elijah, as remarkable a creation as he and they are. But what meager stuff we have on that ministry puts it consistently in a context of crisis as severe for its ninth century B.C. setting as ours in these waning years of the twentieth A.D. How does the consciousness of crisis affect a North American ministry that quite apparently up to the present has been conducted in and on the plateau?

Now the famine was critical in Samaria; the crisis was severe.

The text before us, 1 Kings 18, begins with the promise of rain and ends in fact with the relief of the drought. The three sections of the chapter deal centrally, successively, and brilliantly with three persons, two altars, and one priest.

THREE PERSONS: VV. 2b-19

In the preceding chapter we remarked the narrator's skill in conveying character and personality in the response of person to situation and of person to person. The first section of this chapter is in three brief scenes in which persons, simply and wholly as persons, respond under consciousness of urgency to the critical situation and/or to each other.

Ahab and Obadiah: vv. 2b-6

The famine was critical in Samaria; the crisis was severe. King and First Chancellor, President and Chief of Staff as it were, or, in the ecclesiastical establishment, Minister (or, you should excuse the expression, Senior Minister) and Chairperson of the Board or the congregation themselves and in person take on work deemed under the old "normal" conditions of life on the plateau to be the appropriate task of lesser persons, persons of lower rank or, as we have always preferred to say, persons who do not have to bear the heavy responsibilities that are ours. No less an Old Testament scholar than Hermann Gunkel insisted that this notice has to be a piece of pure legend:

> Die Sage stellt sich in ihrer Kindlichkeit vor, Ahab habe in eigener Person Zusammen mit seinem höchsten Minister Futter für die Rosse gesucht; wofür der geschichtliche Ahab doch wohl geringere Beamte gehabt hätte.[10]

How naïve, Gunkel argues, to represent the king and his highest-ranking minister out looking for feed for the horses themselves, since the historical Ahab certainly had lower-ranking staff for such a task! But this is Israel, not Phoenicia; the United States, not South Africa; this is the people of Yahweh, not the people of Baal; this is the Church, not the State. And it is *drought* in Israel, where horses, and no doubt people, are dying; as it is crisis in our land and on our earth, where people, good people, innocent people, in appalling numbers and proportions are hope-less and, in essence, life-less.

If it was legitimate on the plateau to pull ministerial rank, or to preach and live as if there existed a kind of clean Christian rank for all of us in the church, we know now that this may not be in Israel in drought, in the church-in-the-world under conditions of sustained exigency. The Word of God and the word of earth are met in us, and we are left without rank. We go ourselves in search of green grass and of such means as may alleviate the ravages of an earth whose prevalent systems are advantageous for so few and demeaning and destructive for so many.

And we will have our own critics who will tell us that this is naïve and childish; that in real history it will always be given to some to live with death and to us, by the grace and calling of God, to *live*. But what of Yahweh, what of Christ—in whose presence we exist? What of the biblical faith in which we stand? What of the Word of God and the word of earth—which is the Word of the Cross? Whatever the past, ministry *now* demands that *we* ourselves take to the dirty, dangerous roads on behalf of life that is in jeopardy.

We will find Elijah there.

Obadiah and Elijah: vv. 7-15

Shift identification now in the second scene. It is Obadiah and Elijah. It is parishioner and minister. And God be praised that in the midst of crisis and even the near presence of death, there is place for playful imagination, for humor, for laughter, for caricature, for irreverance, for wild hyperbole—and in all of this, and because of it all, an implicit display of human affection. If on that hard, irrecoverable ground of facticity somewhere underlying the story, the historical Elijah heard such a marvelously creative, whimsical outburst from the historical Obadiah, then Elijah must have laughed aloud before he reassured Obadiah with an oath that he would by God face the king that day! Of course if the narrator had originally informed us of Elijah's pleasure and amusement in Obadiah's superbly comic performance, subsequent traditionists would have removed the notice as out of keeping with the proper character of a proper prophet. In any case it would not have survived down to this day. Some years ago at Yale I introduced to a visiting European biblical scholar one of my own Ph.D. students who was writing a dissertation on humor in the Old Testament. When I said this to my distinguished colleague, he froze in horror and said indignantly, "What humor?"

In our own expression of ministry as we are living it, as we will live it, we will laugh and let laugh. And to my ordained colleagues I say, since it is in God's presence that we exist or, more literally, before whose face we are standing, there is no essential difference in our stance before an Obadiah or before the altar; and quite deliberately I seize this moment of the text to urge that in preaching and in the conduct of public worship, laughter be permitted, encouraged, elicited. Every one of us in the business knows the occasional inevitable liturgical goof. God is better praised by our capitalizing on it than by the pious attempt to gloss it over. Not all but most sermons miss the chance to strike a blow for the kingdom that do not at some point hold up for general laughter some quality of the familiar common life of our time and place.

I'm saying of humor, love it, cherish it, cultivate it, even and especially when you yourself are the quality upheld. The Elijahs and Obadiahs both are better able to live with each other, and particularly under straitened circumstances, when laughter is a constant companion of total ministry.

Elijah and Ahab: vv. 16-19

Here it is Elijah and Ahab: prophet and king; minister and establishment—or structure, or system, or institution; or church and state. Let me reiterate the authenticity, the authority, of the Elijah model. In the traditions of Judaism he is ranked second only to Moses. The impression that he made on his contemporaries and on succeeding generations down to the Christian era and beyond is eloquently attested, of course, in the narratives that we are addressing; in the stories and legends about him in 2 Kings (1 and 2) and 2 Chronicles (21:12ff.); in the remarkable word of Malachi (4:5f.) that before the "great and terrible" Day of Yahweh, Elijah will come to heal the alienation between parents and children; in the praise heaped on him by Ben Sirach in Ecclesiasticus (48:1-11), culminating in the couplet, "Happy are those who saw you/and were honoured with your love!" (so NEB); in repeated references reflecting unsurpassed esteem in apocalyptic tradition (e.g., Rev. 11:3ff.) and in the Gospels where, among other tributes, Elijah, Moses, and Christ are the three transfigured images on the Mount; of course also in Talmudic and Midrashic sources; and in the fact of Elijah's annual dramatic "reappearance" during Judaism's celebration of the Seder.

In broad-ranging, informed consensus, he is not so much the last of the preclassical prophets as he is the first of that phenomenal succession which continues, then, in the next century in Amos, Hosea, and Isaiah. Hermann Gunkel, in a sense the unique father of us all in modern biblical scholarship, despite his insistence on saga's supervision of the Elijah narratives as we receive them, nevertheless affirms on the one hand Elijah's kinship with the greatest of all ministers of ancient Israel, Moses, in their mutual contention with their own people; and, on the other hand, Elijah's legitimate and immediate relationship to the great prophets who follow him and who, essentially, continue the work he began.[11]

The precise phrase that Ahab uses in greeting Elijah does not occur again in subsequent prophetic narratives, but the sense of it conveys the consistent, prevailing annoyance, irritation, frustration, anger, or hostility of king and people—can we say politicians and middle Israelites?—toward the prophet (or the prophetic church): "You troubler of Israel, you!"

In such a matter as this, it may be that no one may call the terms for another, no ministering person for any other minister, no citing of attributes for ministry in general from one's own assessment of general ministry. But you will let me speak personally and say that I do not see how ministry that presumes to honor the prophetic model, as at least in part determinative of the role, can be fulfilled without drawing intermittently but persistently the same essential charge. The worship of Baal, in middle Israel or in middle America (we should say middle USA), is rampant. It is what Paul called the exchange of "the splendour of immortal God for an image shaped like mortal man [Rom. 1:23, NEB]." In this world, in this time; in ministry responsive to the Word of God and the word of earth; in a nation and a church in which it is as if there were no Sermon on the Mount; in such a time of durable earth crisis, we will not only be called troublers of Israel, we will be in Ahab's sense troublers of Israel.

And we of the faith will have to have the courage to do what Elijah did, that is, fling the epithet back in the accusers' teeth[12]: It is not I who have troubled Israel, but you and your father's house, you and your kind, you and your acquisitive systems. It was not the draft-and-war resisters who were troublers of Israel, but you the guardians of structures of racism, of imperialism, of exploitation. It is not Cesar Chavez and his union that have troubled Israel, but you and your devices of callousness and greed which hold in subhuman servitude the life of farm-working Chicano families from young to old. It is not militant Blacks; it is not aggrieved, bitter native Americans; it is not a newly assertive breed of women; it is not the alienated, intellectual radical left who are troublers of these states of ours, but us, U.S., we, all of us of relative power, who let the dream for all of us become a nightmare for all of them. Prophet/Minister, to people and nation: Not I (or maybe even I?) but you and your father's ways are troublers of the earth.

A great contemporary Elijah, Archbishop Dom Helder Camara of Brazil, urges on us all the creation of "a world that is more breathable."[13] It is not he, or the vast majority of Brazilians, but a few of them, in part under our demonic tutelage, that create and preserve there and similarly in other parts of the earth the nonbreathable world, the miserable conditions of human suffocation.

Three persons: Ahab, Obadiah, Elijah. Ahab to Obadiah: We'll do it ourselves. Obadiah to Elijah: You're a spook, buddy! Elijah to Ahab: Troubler of Israel—not I, but you. Word of God, word of earth. Ministry.

TWO ALTARS: VV. 20-40

In the center of this scene stand two altars, one of Yahweh, one of Baal.[14] The issue of the Carmel convocation is drawn, not by the desertion of one for the other, not by the defection of Yahwists to Baalism, but by the widely held assumption in Yahwist Israel that Yahwism may also embrace Baalism and that one may worship at the Baal altar and at the same time remain Yahwist. In the course of the scene Elijah repairs the Yahweh altar (the primary sense of the Hebrew verb here is that he "healed" the altar) which had been ruined—we can only guess—perhaps by an act of religious vandalism, or by neglect, or indeed immediately in the course of the frenetic, violent performance of the Baal prophets. Elijah understands that the two altars may not stand in the same sanctuary and that the Baal altar may not be honored without tacit denial of Yahweh and the prostitution of the faith of Israel. His own prophetic passion comes to a boil over the accommodation of Yahwism to Baalism. How long will you go on believing that you can be Yahwist when you are also Baalist?

Professor von Rad comments on the scene:

It must have come as a great surprise to [the Carmel Convocation] that Elijah viewed the matter as a case of "either-or." At the time no one else saw as he did that there was no possibility of accommodation between the worship of Baal and Israel's ancient Jahwistic traditions. . . . [For Elijah] the co-existence, or rather the coalescence, of the two forms of worship, in which the rest of the people were perfectly at home, was intolerable.[15]

"Coalescence" is a good word for it. Elijah's address to the Carmel assembly begins with a question, enigmatic in the Hebrew, which I have translated, "How long will you go on vacillating between the two alternatives (that is, Yahweh and Baal)?"[16]

> *The Revised Standard Version* reads: How long will you go limping with two different opinions?
> *The Jerusalem Bible:* How long do you mean to hobble first on one leg then on the other?
> *The New American Bible:* How long will you straddle the issue?
> *The New English Bible:* How long will you sit on the fence?[17]
> Montgomery's Commentary on Kings (ICC): How long are you hobbling . . . *at the two forks* (of the road), i.e., hopping now on one leg, now on the other, before the dilemma. . . . Elijah is here using some popular phrase.[18]
> And Skinner's commentary: The literal sense of the Hebrew is obscure, but the idea of the question is clear from what immediately follows. It satirizes the attempt to combine two religions so incongruous as those of Baal and Yahweh.[19]

However rendered, this is the perennial prophetic question which was and still must be addressed unceasingly to the institutionalized manifestations of the biblical faith whose easy coalescence with Baal worship takes place whenever and wherever that faith becomes provincialized, parochialized, and accommodated to the culture in such a way that the adherents lose altogether the sense of critical distinction between Yahweh and Baal, between the Word of God and the word of persons, between the word of earth and the word of the system, between God who is and god who is made, God who creates and god who is created—in sum, between God and his cultural image or, more bluntly, between Christ and mammon. Jesus said, "You cannot serve both," knowing full well that this was precisely the prevailing religious situation of his own people. He spoke prophetically.[20]

In her series of essays entitled *Liberation Theology*, Rosemary Ruether cites in several contexts the fourth-century alliance, mutually beneficent in certain respects, between Constantinian Rome and Palestinian Christianity. She writes that it is

> the ambiguity [How long will you vacillate between the two alternatives] and tragedy of Christianity [that] a faith with roots in revolutionary messianic hope . . . was co-opted into the imperialist ideology and social structure of the later Roman empire. . . . Christianity itself was used to sanctify and perpetuate the hierarchical society and world view of classical culture.[21]

For the church it was of course a kind of alliance which has been repeated and reinforced down to this moment. This ambiguity and tragedy in all the institutional expressions of biblical faith may be in some measure always and inevitably present. The process of coalescence, of accommodation, of succumbing to co-optation is to some degree continuous, and it must be therefore continuously exposed, challenged, and checked. This is of the essence of prophetic ministry, a ministry never *done*, never completed.

This process, this working tendency toward the coalescence of Yahweh and Baal, can be observed in almost any church in this country, in almost any pulpit, in almost any pew. We will not agree, perhaps, as to where or in whom a patently co-opted faith, an ambiguous Christianity, appears most conspicuously, most tragically; but many of us are painfully aware of it in some of the most popular, widely heard, sometimes lionized clergy of our time. I think it is true of them and their hearers, as apparently it was in the Israel of Elijah and Ahab, that they really do not know the extent to which their Word of God has been twisted, tortured, and adulterated by its possibly innocent and unconscious fusion with the word of decent, respectable, prosperous, white, capitalist, North American woman and man. The biblical faith, with roots in revolutionary messianic hope which is itself rooted in the prophetism of ancient Israel/Judah, is even now, and daily, used to sanctify and perpetuate the life, culture, security, and privilege not now of imperialist Rome but of the imperialist United States.

Is it possible that the presence of the flag of the United States of America *in the sanctuary* of the church signifies the coalescence of Yahweh and Baal, of Christ and culture? In other settings that flag may represent our best and highest national achievements and aspirations. But I can't escape the feeling that *in the church,* the national flag betrays again the ambiguity and tragedy of contemporary biblical faith, rooted in revolutionary messianic hope but, alas, comfortably accommodated to the self-seeking ways of an inevitably corrupted temporal state.

From time to time I am compelled to address myself to that vastly overworked, unresolved, often heatedly controverted subject of the relationship of the seminary to the church. Some in the church tend to believe that the seminary—at least "liberal" interdenominational seminaries like ours—are, with horrendous results, hopelessly detached from the realities of the workaday world and—such is the mind of our most bitter (and most reactionary) critics—that our graduates are rendered in fact maladroit if not downright incompetent by the very training designed to fit them for ministry. They become fit, if they do at all, only when prudent, mature lay and other clergy minds already in the church prevail over them, and when the hard realities of the church in this particular capitalist society are beaten into them. Precisely.

I suppose I have already suggested how some of us in the seminary tend to see the church. On the whole, I'm optimistic about the increasing détente between church and seminary and, at the same time, over the mutual creativity and productivity of the inevitably continuing tension in their intimate, indispensable relationship. As a consummately biblically oriented seminarian, I remain unalterably persuaded of one requisite quality in the relationship. The seminary must remain in some sense prophet to the church. The one thing we may not do in seminary is send out into the church clergy who do not know the difference between the two altars and who, in the language of the model, bless the altar of Baal in the name of Yahweh, or the enterprises of the system in the name of Jesus Christ. The seminary must purify itself and the church against the unceasing incursions of Baal. But it would be oversimplification if not institutional idolatry to suggest that the seminary play in fact the very role of Elijah to the contemporary church of the two altars. God knows the seminary has its own dual or multiple altars to work through and around. I can tell you that my recent moments of greatest frustration and discouragement have been on that recurrent June day when I have handed an M.Div. diploma to a young, bright graduate who has nevertheless survived four years of college and three years of seminary unemancipated from the prevailing cultural slavery, unawakened to the word of anguished earth, indiscriminate between the Word of God and the word of the nation, undisturbed by, or even unaware of, the urgency of prophetism, and apparently innocent of the radical and loving, ruthless and merciful, devastating and redeeming claim of the gospel upon us. That claim *is* Elijah to us and the church: "How long will you go on in this egregious fusion of Yahweh and Baal?" How long, how long?

All of us in our varied ministries tend to be awed by the structures and potency of the establishment of Baal, even though we know, somewhere down there in the timid, secret resources of faith, that *all* the stuff of Baal doesn't make God—power, technological sophistication, machismo, sex, political, military, and economic domination, energy independence (ha!). Out of Baal, even at high noon (which is right now) with all his desperate, violent prophets screaming around his altar—out of Baal we really know, don't we, that there will be no sound, no response; no voice, no answer, nor even any sign of attention. The fire that lights the sacrifice and kindles worship, and the Word that creates, judges, and redeems, is not there.

In the Elijah model, part of the work of ministry is the courageous, authentic appropriation and imposition of the taunt of Elijah (v. 27) upon ourselves, upon the seminary, and upon the respective constituencies of our ministry. It is the staid, very scholarly, very proper *International Critical Commentary* that best describes it. "Elijah's satire in a nutshell is the raciest comment ever made on Pagan mythology."[22] Here too is high, if off-color, humor in the Elijah stories, this time from Elijah himself. Sure Baal is God; a meditating, trip-taking, sleeping-waking, and—in the midst of all that, dropped as it were casually—toilet-going God! Pagan mythology it is, ensconced in our time and embraced in our church, where we have supposed that we can know the glory of immortal God while worshiping also at the altar of our powerful and overwhelmingly impressive national Baal, an image, in the final analysis, simply made by human minds and hands.

In the first draft of this chapter, before I had really worked this section freshly through again, I concluded the discussion of the text of 1 Kings 18:20-40 with this conventionally pious and liberal comment:

> I reject vehemently [I wrote] and out of hand the last verse of this section [v. 40]: "Elijah said to the people, 'Seize the prophets of Baal; let none of them escape.' They seized them; and Elijah led them down to the Wadi Kishon and slaughtered them there." [Then I went on to say] I quite understand the ancient, binding custom of what is called the "ban" by the imposition of which, as the Jerusalem Bible apologetically footnotes, "in this war be-

tween Yahweh and Baal those who serve Baal suffer the fate of the conquered in the warfare of the times." But [I said in this earlier draft] it is an utterly time-bound notice, and its value in the text is, for us, sharply negative.

I take it back now. I took it back. Again, I cannot presume to make for anyone else the precise contemporary interpretation of the notice of the slaughter of the Baal prophets; but this awful scene, whatever the facts underlying it,[23] is absolutely coherent with and essential to what has gone before. Elijah denies us the course of courteous rapprochement by which, the sermon preached, the Word spoken (as we believe and hope), the "victory" won, we shake hands all around—and continue to live with the two altars. That's what prophets and ministers in the biblical faith—with all too uncommon exception—have been doing for thousands of years.

If now Elijah's drought of the moment ends, our essential situation of crisis appears to be continuous in our future. A *radical* break is called for, a radical separation of the two altars and a radical renewal of the biblical faith. In and of themselves, these lines of slaughter are horrible. We do not want to hear them or translate them or, in whatever way appropriate to our own time and ethic, act upon them. But there it is, and it is a "true" word, if we "translate" it sensitively. "Elijah said *to the people,* 'Seize the prophets of Baal; let none of them escape.' They seized them; and Elijah led them down to the Wadi Kishon and slaughtered them there."

God grant that no one reading this take me to be condoning for our own time any such violence, to say nothing of slaughter. The sense of the model for us is the urgency of the imperative: Break, totally and radically, with Baal!

ONE PRIEST: VV. 41-46

I think one cannot find in Hebrew prose
A passage more poetically conceived
And executed. In its choice of words
As in its structure, it is unsurpassed.

Elijah said to Ahab, "Stir yourself,
Take food and drink; because I hear the swish
Of rain." So Ahab went to eat and drink.
But not Elijah; climbing to the top
Of Carmel, crouching on the ground with face

Between his knees, he asked his servant, "Now
Go out and look across the sea." He went.
"But there is nothing there at all," he said;
So, seven times Elijah sent him back.
The seventh time the servant said, "Yes sir!
I see a cloud no bigger than a hand
Arising from the sea." Elijah said,
"Go quick, tell Ahab, 'Harness up and move,
Before the rain prevents you!'"

     All the while
The skies grew dark with clouds, the wind arose—
Then heavy rain. Mounting his chariot,
The king made for Jezreel. By Yahweh's might
The prophet pulled himself together; and,
As runner to the chariot, he went
With Ahab all the way to Jezreel's gate.

The prophet/minister is one—one priest
Who must be minister and priest to all.

What does this say to ordained ministry,
In crisis now sustained and durable?
What now of ministry for those of us
Who serve the "better" churches of the land?
What now of ministry to royalty,
To those who eat and drink and ride about
In mighty chariots; who know no hurt
Though drought and famine stalk the earth
And decimate the human family;
Who do not know, or will not face the fact,
That their secure existence is maintained
At frightful cost to all the dispossessed?

How, minister to royalty, who call
The prophets troublers of the church,
Disturbers of the Christian peace, meddlers
In matters—so they say—irrelevant
To life in faith and hope and love; for whom
The double altar is imperative;
Who seek to shape the deity in form
That sanctifies the royal of the earth?

What then of ministry to royalty—
Since quite precisely it is these to whom
We minister? Indeed, we have to say,
We've met the royalty and they are us!

The prophet/minister is one—one priest
Who must be minister and priest to all.
Elijah does not cut himself adrift
From them; he does not cry a plague on them
And on their fathers' house—not yet at least.
One commentator notes Elijah's courtesy
"In bidding monarch to refresh himself."[24]
But while it is the wont of royalty
To eat and drink, the prophet/minister,
Close to the word of earth and sensitive
To Word of God, searches and waits for sign
And way of blessing of the families
Of earth, of sweet relief from poverty,
Injustice, and oppression—from the drought
Of inhumanity and misery.

The prophet/minister is one—one priest
Who must be minister and priest to all.
We minister among the royalty.
We serve the Word of God and word of earth.
Numbered among oppressors, in the main,
Are our constituents, whom we must hold
In love and understanding, though we know
The royal ways.

                    We do not enter, then,
Their chariots, but run somehow along,
In touch with them, beside them, holding on.
By Yahweh's might, his hand on us, we keep
Our own integrity and work to see
The single Yahweh altar in the church.

The prophet/minister is one—one priest
Who must be minister and priest to all.

III
THE CAVE:
1 KINGS 19

Virtually all modern scholars in all the surviving biblical faiths (except, of course, those of essentially fundamentalist persuasion) are agreed that the four primary Elijah narratives (1 Kings 17—19,21) have suffered intrusion, alteration, and expansion in the long centuries of transmission before they became unalterably fixed in the early years of our own Common Era.

Here is the narrative of the Cave (1 Kings 19) as it may first have come to form, oral or written, still in Elijah's own century. The reading is reconstructed from the present Hebrew text in consultation with other primary versions and translations, and out of respect for the critical judgments of major scholars of this century. At the same time, I hope it is not necessary for me to say I do not believe that this or any other comparable effort may lay claim to the precisely literal recovery of the text as it was first given determinative form by the genius of the original Elijah narrator(s). This, one knows, is an achievement that may never be.

It is, however, clear that the story is now disfigured, not only by would-be "improvers" of the textual tradition but also by an indiscriminate fusion in the popular mind of the Elijah and Elisha images and narratives. One has only to compare the two literary parallels (there are no more) in the two cycles of stories—those of the flour and oil, and of the widow's son—to be aware of the historical and conceptual chasm that separates them. The Elisha parallels are a rank and, of course, insubstantial imitation—one has to say, again in quotes, "improvement"—of the Elijah episodes, designed to represent Elisha as the greater miracle worker. Indeed, even subsequent Elijah traditionists have touched the narratives here and there so as to say to the rival Elisha people, "But you see, our prophet too was quite a miracle worker!"

In the four chapters of 1 Kings that are in the main the creation of the Elijah narrator, we meet a highly gifted verbalist, who is given to the use of unique words, forms, and structures; who is relatively sophisticated; who, as compared with the Elisha narrators, for example, appears to be notably disinterested in miracle for the sake of miracle; and who shares with Elijah himself a kind of precognition of the substance of classical prophetism.

His work ranks with the finest classical Hebrew prose to be found anywhere in the Old Testament, displaying a phenomenal verbal/literary technique in the use of humor and irony, in subtle, sensitive character portrayal, and in effective, varied appeal to human emotion. And in the reconstruction and/or creation of dialogue, the Elijah narrator is unsurpassed.

Here, then, a critical reconstruction of the narrative of the Cave.

On the Way to the Cave: 1 Kings 19:2-6a, 8

2 Now Jezebel sent this word to Elijah: "If you are Elijah, I am
3 Jezebel!" Frightened for his life, he ran away; and when he got
to Beersheba in Judah, he left his servant there and went on
4 himself for a day into the wilderness; until at last he sat down
under a broom tree and prayed that he might die. "I've had it,
Yahweh," he said. "Take my life: I'm no better than those
5 who've gone before me." He lay down there and went to sleep;
until suddenly someone touched him and said, "Wake up and
6a eat." He looked about—and there at his head was a stone-
8 baked biscuit and a jar of water. So he ate and drank and then,
on the strength of that nourishment, he went on to Horeb.

The Stay at the Cave: 1 Kings 19:9a, 11b, 12-15, 18

9a Coming there to a cave, he spent the night.

11b And there was a mighty wind
Not in the wind was Yahweh

And after the wind, earthquake
Not in the earthquake was Yahweh

12 And after the earthquake, fire
Not in the fire was Yahweh

And after the fire—
A sound of gentle silence.

13 Upon hearing this, Elijah covered his face with his robe and
went out to take his position at the mouth of the cave. It was
only now that the Word of Yahweh *was:* "What are you doing
14 here, Elijah?" Elijah replied: "I have been passionately devoted to Yahweh, God of hosts, even while the people of Israel
have abandoned you. Your altars they have destroyed, your
prophets they have put to death with the sword. I am left now,
15a myself, alone; and they are after me to take my life!" But
Yahweh answered him, "Go back the way you have come;
18 because there are still seven thousand left in Israel whose
knees have never bent to Baal, nor whose lips have kissed
him!"

The Way Back from the Cave: 1 Kings 19:19-21

19 Leaving that place [Elijah] came upon Elisha son of Shaphat plowing with twelve yoke of oxen in front of him, and he with the twelfth. As Elijah passed by, he tossed his robe over him.

20 Leaving the oxen, [Elisha] ran after Elijah and said, "Let me give my father and mother a farewell kiss; then I will follow you." Elijah said to him, "Go on back: what claim have I got

21 over you?" Leaving him, Elisha went back, took the pair of oxen, slaughtered them, used the implements [of plowing] to cook their flesh, and gave [it] to the people to eat. Then he left to follow Elijah, and he became his disciple.

It is, of course, our story: the threat, real or simply paranoid; the flight in terror through the wilderness of despair; the wonder of sustenance in the desert; the darkness, the stillness, the strangely comforting loneliness of the cave in which we spend a night or a week or however long it takes for the noise and fury of our hell to subside; the perception of the gift, now, of gentle silence; the miracle, then, of the discovery anew of the "isness" of the Word, but the immediate, bitter protest against it because it will not let us stay in this place of haven from storm, this realm of the silence of gentleness, because it sends us back again, and because it rebukes the pride of our paranoia, our monumental sense of absolutely unique commitment and persecution; and finally our return, to call an Elisha on the way and to resume the work of ministry to Word of God and word of earth, renewed by the whole kaleidoscopic experience of the trip to the Cave.

ON THE WAY TO THE CAVE: VV. 2-6a, 8

(V.2)   Now Jezebel sent this word to Elijah: "If you are Elijah, I am Jezebel!"

This is verse 2 of the chapter. With very considerable critical support, verse 1 is omitted as a secondary and artificial link between chapters 17-18 and chapter 19. The present verse 1 reports that Ahab told the whole Carmel story to Jezebel. I don't protest the order of the chapters but suspect, along with a lot of others who've worked this through, that this Cave narrative was originally independent of the sequences of the drought in 17-18. And Jezebel's message is as it is preserved in the Septuagint, the Greek translation of Hebrew scripture completed in the closing centuries of the pre-Christian era. That text presupposes the magnificent and, one suspects, authentic Hebrew line: "If you are Elijah, then I am Jezebel"; you may be a prophet, but I am royalty; your name may mean "God is Yahweh," but as long as I'm here neither you nor Yahweh will stand in the kingdom of this royal house!

Make your own appropriations. Here are some of mine. It's a beautiful Saturday morning in Nanking. I'm attending Hillcrest American School and boarding with a missionary couple near retirement, their kids long since grown. It's a matter of dispute between them and me whether I'm supposed to practice the piano on Saturday. I haven't this morning. I've gone out to play. I'm ten years old. Mrs. Wilson, furious, calls me into the house. "If you are Davie, I am Mrs. Wilson." My parents are summoned from Chinkiang, two hours by rail down the Yangtze, and I am put to bed on bread and water for the rest of the weekend. (I am devastated for Saturday, but secretly I do not mind missing the long Sunday in church.) The trip to the Cave was real, but short.

Years later, 1939. I am in seminary, third year, Christmas vacation near. Failing vision in my left eye; detachment of the retina; immediate operation at Johns Hopkins and possible abandonment of projected Ph.D. program in Old Testament. "If you are Davie, I am Adversity." The trip to the Cave was longer.

It is the late 1940s. I am the teaching chaplain at the University of Georgia. It is, of course, before the Supreme Court decision of 1954 and the Martin Luther King era of the 1960s. My wife, Joy, and I host a seminar of mine—all white, of course—for dinner and, as it turned out, a very long evening's discussion with three black Morehouse faculty, George Kelsey in Christian Ethics, A. E. Jones in French, and Ed Williams in Economics. An influential university colleague learns of it and confronts me in fury: "You *ate* with niggers? I'll have you fired if it's the last thing I do!" If you are Davie, I am Bill. (Even, then, he couldn't do it: Dr. Harmon Caldwell, then president, stood firm and, for the time, courageously in my support.)

Now it is the 1950s. I am on the faculty of the Yale Divinity School, collaborating with a colleague at another seminary on what is to be a jointly written introduction to the Old Testament. Suddenly in the midst of the venture he writes, in effect, Your stuff is too inferior to mine to be published with it. "If you are Davie, I am (shall we say) Egbert." On that one too I went to the Cave, where the Word, and my wife, Joy, and my colleague, Richard Niebuhr, sent me back to publish that same stuff in my first book, *From Faith to Faith*.

It is 1967. I am an outspoken university chaplain and I have offended the university's conservative constituency, including the president. The very simple message: "If you are the chaplain, I am the president." The issue then centered in Vietnam, the bitter opposition to it and its effects by the vast majority of students, and the role of the chapel as the center of the resistance. Years later, when he was no longer president and I was on my way elsewhere, but US personnel were still waging the war, he dropped by my office, fell glumly into a chair, and said, "Davie, what are we going to do about this damned war?"

This is to illustrate, autobiographically, something of the variety of the form of the trauma, Elijah/Jezebel, that may send us, running for life as it were, through the desert to the cave.

(Vv. 3-4)   *Frightened for his life, he [Elijah] ran away; and when he got to Beersheba in Judah, he left his servant there and went on himself for a day into the wilderness; until at last he sat down under a broom tree and prayed that he might die. "I've had it, Yahweh," he said. "Take my life: I'm no better than those who've gone before me."*

Elijah: God person, Yahweh prophet, drought manager, theological persuader—this Elijah is terrified, literally scared out of his wits and running for his life. It is interesting and understandable that in the history of Elijah tradition, "fear" was changed to "awareness"— a simple alteration in vowels in Hebrew—so that the mighty prophet is represented as running away not because he is frightened but because he "sees"; he is prudently aware of Jezebel's implicit threat. Elijah's fear only serves to bring him closer to us. Our *being* in ministry—as Elijah and his narrators know very well—provides us in the faith with neither doubtlessness nor fearlessness, and our total ministry, like Elijah's, is enhanced by our acknowledgment of full susceptibility to all the natural shocks that flesh and faith are heir to.

Some suggest that Elijah is suicidal.[1] I wonder. There may well be a little Semitic-Oriental hyperbole here, as also in the Moses saga, when Moses says, If this is the way it is to be, then take my life.[2] Elijah is devastated, in despair, and shattered. He knows the not uncharacteristic prophetic wish, then and now, to be derobed, demantled, defrocked. You can have the whole thing, Yahweh, he says. Carry on, Yahweh—but count me out. Go ahead with your fight, but *ohne mich*. And dear God, don't we all know this! So let's get it out, with a proper prayer, not a conventionally pious prayer like, you know, "O Lord, I'm courageous; only help thou mine uncourage." We ought to be able to say, "Yahweh, eternal God, Lord of my Lord Jesus Christ, I've had all of Jezebel I can stand! Get her off my back! And if you can't do that, then I say the whole deal stinks, and I want out! I've had it, Yahweh. I'm no better than my mothers, my fathers, my ancestors, those who have gone before me. It is enough. . . . Take my life, since, God knows, I am not better than they."

(Vv. 5,6a,8) *He lay down there and went to sleep; until suddenly someone touched him and said, "Wake up and eat." He looked about—and there at his head was a stone-baked biscuit and a jar of water. So he ate and drank and then, on the strength of that nourishment, he went on to Horeb.*

The present text reads, by later insertion, that Elijah went "forty days and forty nights" to Horeb. This is a well-meaning but bungling and imprecise transfer from the saga of Moses, who spent forty days and forty nights on the sacred mountain.[3] This notice nevertheless testifies to the judgment of tradition that Elijah is in rank comparable to Moses.

Here we go again. Improbable ravens improbably feed us in the wadi of a dying stream. Preposterously, we are sustained in the home of a widow, herself and her son on the verge of death by starvation. How perverse of us, dearly beloved, that we are, as we are, in terror! And now, in this desert of despair, despondent enough to be at least *talking* suicide, someone—thank God for someone— who was it, and who told this someone of my presence here, and of my deathlike discouragement?—someone *touched* me, woke me out of my dreams of desertion and death, spoke to me face to face, voice to ear, person to person, and gave me food and drink. Someone. Thank God for someone!

It is a fact of our condition in ministry, indeed a fact of the condition of faith, that we will be sustained in ways all but incredible—no, really incredible—even in our flight in terror through the wilderness of despair.

And it *is* "someone"; not, as the later, present expansion of the text would have it, "someone, an angel." This appositional intrusion of orthodox piety enters the text at verse 5 some time after the simple, grace-full mystery of the original narrative had already been "clarified" with the addition of verses 6b and 7. These lines are added for the sake of the role of the angel and to accord the proper deference due this prophetic patriarch. According to this insertion, Elijah goes back to sleep again, to be awakened a second time not by an indefinite "someone" but by an angel of Yahweh; and this time the prophet is not only fed but verbally, sentimentally, romantically soothed: Eat now, sweet prophet, because you've got to make it all the way to the Cave! If we know what it is to live on raven food and widow fare, we can accept gracefully the grace of God from any "someone" who proffers it. The "someone" of the original text in any case makes a better angel.

Consistently now, the fare of ministry-in-crisis is or ought to be simple, modest, perhaps even frugal—although how many of us can lay claim to that? Here, it is water to drink; and to eat, a biscuit, a scone, a small piece of dough baked on the hot stones. The Hebrew word is *'ugah,* and we get some notion of its meagerness when Hosea denounces Ephraim as a little piece of dough cooked on only one side; literally, a half-baked *'ugah.*[4]

It is, of course, the profound point of this scene of the narrative that on the strength, if need be in crisis, only of a little bread and water, Elijah and we go on to Horeb.

THE STAY AT THE CAVE: VV. 9a, 11b, 12-15a, 18

(V. 9a) *Coming there [Mount Horeb] to a cave, he spent the night.*

If we may presume now to clear away editorial additions from subsequent traditionists whose spontaneous but misconceived aim it was to enhance the splendor of the theophany and bring it into conformity with Mosaic saga,[5] then we have before us a description that is incomparably eloquent by virtue precisely of economy, simplicity, and, in all of biblical literature, stark singularity. Time stands quite still. It is a moment of crisis majestically detached from all known and common ways, and it is recounted in Hebrew without the use of a single verb to sap the naked power of static, substantive words. We can get by in English using only the imperfect of the verb "to be," but the Hebrew remains starker, barer, more powerful, more arresting:

(V. 11b)   *There was a mighty wind*
Not in the wind was Yahweh

And after the wind earthquake
Not in the earthquake was Yahweh

(V. 12)   *And after the earthquake fire*
Not in the fire was Yahweh

And after the fire—
A sound of gentle silence.

This reading omits, again with nearly unanimous critical support, verses 9b-10, an almost identical duplication of verses 13b-14. The question "What are you doing here, Elijah?" and his response are appropriate only *after* he emerges from the cave. The command of 11a to "stand before Yahweh" is also premature; and what immediately follows in 11a, the notice that "Yahweh passed by," is an import from Mosaic theophanies where Yahweh manifests himself in these very physical phenomena:

Now at daybreak on the third day there were peals of thunder on the mountain and lightning flashes, a dense cloud, and a loud trumpet blast. . . . The mountain [of Sinai (= Horeb)] was entirely wrapped in smoke, because Yahweh had descended on it in the form of fire. Like smoke from a furnace the smoke went up, and the whole mountain shook violently. . . . Moses spoke, and God answered with peals of thunder.

[Again] Moses said, "Show me your glory, I beg you." And [Yahweh] said, "I will let all my splendour pass in front of you. . . . You cannot see my face . . . for [one] cannot see me and live. . . . [But] here is a place beside me. You must stand on the rock, and when my glory passes by, I will put you in a cleft of the rock and shield you with my hand while I pass by. Then I will take my hand away and you shall see the back of me; but my face is not to be seen."[6]

The command to Elijah to stand before Yahweh while Yahweh passes by, as well as the phrases which enhance the violence of the wind in verse 11, are accretions all but irresistibly motivated by the fact of the coincidence of the Sinai-Horeb theophanies and by tradition's firm establishment of a kind of Moses-Elijah parity.

But all this serves only to create a contradiction in the narrative of Elijah, where we have to do not with a cleft in the rock but with the Cave, and where it is the emphatic point of the Elijah narrative, the precise point, that in the violent physical phenomena of wind, earthquake, and fire, Yahweh is not only not passing by but that in no sense whatsoever is he even present in these phenomena. One suspects that the narrative stands as a splendid rebuke to all of those (or any of us) nature worshipers who are episodically disposed to make a theophany out of natural phenomena from sex to sunset, mountain to sea, rose to artichoke.[7]

Alas, dear hearts, it is not even the still, small voice. When the deafening sound of the awe-full violence of nature is past and there is that sudden, contrasting gentleness of quiet, that audible *voice* of silence, it is the Word of Yahweh (preserved in verse 9a) that *is*, that comes, that occurs, that happens, that is articulate and apprehendable. Since a theophany is "a physical presentation or manifestation of deity . . . a brief *appearance* of deity,"[8] it is a question whether Elijah's experience on the sacred mountain is a theophany at all. Yahweh was not in wind, earthquake, or fire; and after all of these, there was a sound of gentle silence.

(V. 13) *Upon hearing this, Elijah covered his face with his robe and went out to take his position at the mouth of the cave. It was only now that the World of Yahweh was* [that is, that it came, that it occurred, that it happened, that it was articulate and apprehendable]: *"What are you doing here, Elijah?"*

Mah-lecha poh 'eliyahu?

Elijah replied. . . .

Now watch the defense mechanism come into play. Elijah is of course taken aback. He is affronted. What kind of Yahweh Word is this, this implicit rebuff? Doesn't *he* understand that it's this damned prophetic role of *his* that brings me here to the Cave, shattered, exhausted, running and hiding for my very life? I don't need this critical-interrogating Word; I need the healing Word, the affirming Word, the stroking Word.

(V. 14) *Elijah replied* [to that seemingly uninformed, unsympathetic Word, Elijah replied testily]: "*I have been passionately devoted to Yahweh, God of hosts, even while the people of Israel have abandoned you. Your altars they have destroyed, your prophets they have put to death with the sword. I am left now, myself, alone; and they are after me to take my life!*"

One can hear it on occasion from any parish minister in the land: Yahweh's Lone Ranger . . . Horatio at the Bridge . . . Hans Brinker with his silver skates and his finger in the dike (or was that somebody else?) . . . the last single remaining bastion of theological and prophetic integrity . . . and, for background music, the *Tannhaüser Overture*. Don't you understand: *they are after me!*

(V. 15a) *But Yahweh answered [Elijah]: "Go back the way you have come. . . .*

I'm omitting verses 15b, 16, and 17, the tri-commission to anoint two kings and a prophet: Hazael over Syria, Jehu over Israel, and Elisha to succeed Elijah himself. The late Prof. James Montgomery, whose commentary on Kings published post-humously in 1951 under the editorship of Henry Gehman was the last volume in the distinguished series, *The International Critical Commentary*, writes of these verses and the commission:

> This sequel remains a standing puzzle. Elijah did not anoint Hazael and Jehu; it was Elisha [who] suggested to Hazael the murder of his predecessor (II Kings 8:7ff.), and who indirectly anointed Jehu (9:1ff.). The alleged commission to Elijah appears to be a case of transfer from the Elisha legend.[9]

To which I would simply add that even the commission to "anoint" Elisha is spurious: aside from the single instance of Isaiah 61:1, where the reference is probably only metaphorical,[10] there is no evidence whatsoever that the practice of anointing prophets existed in Old Testament Israel.

(Vv. 15a, 18) *Yahweh answered [Elijah]: "Go back the way you have come. . . . Retrace your steps; return to where and what you were because there are still seven thousand left in Israel* [the number is no census count but a round number, "thousands upon thousands"] *whose knees have never bent to Baal, nor whose lips have kissed him!"*

The way to the cave or, to broaden the metaphor, the ways to the caves are as crowded these US years as roads to the beaches on

Labor Day weekend. Why have we become a generation of cave-seekers? Well, if Elijah is legion, then so is Jezebel; and if Jezebel is legion, so is the cave.

As the flight to the cave is undertaken by vast numbers for a vast range of reasons, so too the nature of the cave varies vastly and appropriately. Nevertheless, every search for the cave represents the more or less desperate craving of the searcher for relief from coping with the seemingly uncopeable. The cave is the womb.

A few of the obvious drives that pack us off, daily or weekly or episodically or, for some, in hope, permanently, are fear or even terror in the particular given set of circumstances; the sheer discouragement and exhaustion of facing questions without answer; profound disillusionment—it takes many forms—with the pertinent, prevailing system or systems; deep and bitter contempt for one's own society, bred of the abysmal failure to attain in consistent practice even a semblance of the justice professed and acclaimed; despair—so it was with the college generation of the late sixties—over the formidable obduracy of a political establishment in going its merciless way quite apparently deaf to the cries of anguish of its empathetic and real victims, victims by the tens of millions here and around the world. The Brazilian bishop Dom Helder Camara, in that same Harvard address from which I quoted in the preceding chapter, tells us to "beware of escape mechanisms, conscious or not." And then he calls attention to what is surely in potential one of our most disastrous forms of cavism:

> Beware, especially, of a very serious sign—and here I think, above all, of the admirable youth of today's world: the danger that after the enthusiasm, the dedication without limits, the commitment during university days, they will reach the phase of installation in life, of conformism, of bourgeoisie-ism, of the death of ideals.[11]

"What are you doing here, Elijah?"

The traffic to the cave may embrace us all, rich and poor, royalty and commoner, black and white, free and slave, female and male, peasant and landowner, exploiter and oppressed—and all of us bent on exchanging what we deem to be an unremediable, intolerable, essentially uninhabitable situation for peace—or even the illusion of peace. And the range of caves runs from the old standbys of sex and alcohol and other drugs to TA (Transactional Analysis), TM (Transcendental Meditation), TV (before whom, on an average, we stand, sit, lie, eat, and drink an unconscionable and unbelievable number of adult hours per week), TF (touchy-feely in dual or group encounters), TZ (try Zen), TS (take Sominex), or even, in some circles, TJ (take Jesus—in this sense an icon distantly derived from Jesus Christ), and literally scores of others.

And one more cave in the "T" series, TB—turn back; turn back to the past; if we can't hold it intact in every present we can return to it. I'm told—I don't *know* this—that the most popular song surviving from the Beatles era is "Yesterday." "I believe in yesterday." It is possible to go even farther back into the cave. A San Francisco columnist, writing within days of President Ford's accession, said of him, "He likes things to be the way they were the day before yesterday."

Now, it is not my intention to say that the cave has no legitimate function. Elijah *came back* from the cave revived, renewed. Although the Word of Yahweh appears to have been absent and silent *in* the cave, the experience of the cave, the recapitulation of the womb, the *distance* and *perspective* afforded by the cave from and upon Baalism and Jezebel and Israel—all this was and is a legitimate gift of the legitimate and essential cave trip. It may be given to us, to all Elijahs, to return from the cave with fear and terror, if not allayed, at least in control; with new resources given to face unanswerable questions with courage and endurance; with disillusionment transformed to fresh determination; with societal contempt converted again to sorrow, compassion, and resolution; and with despair turning back once more to prophetic passion.

I hope it is unnecessary to say that both the church and the seminary suffer erosion of authenticity in proportion to the measure of their acquiescence in institutional cave-playing. Many, lay and clergy, would make the church the cave, the escape, the refuge, the womb. The resources of faith, which by the grace of God are imparted to the church as gifts to be given and proclaimed, are themselves such, properly dispensed, as to render infrequent or unnecessary the trip to the cave. But the church itself may not *be* the cave, except at the cost of losing both the Word of God and the word of earth.

So, too, the seminary, where we must look harder and more critically than we have in the past at applicants who are clearly seeking not a theological education but in fact the cave. Dr. John Kildahl, a practicing New York psychoanalyst and an adjunct seminary instructor, believes that we in the seminaries have been admitting too many theological students with high dependency needs and with consequently sustained and often serious psychological problems. He calls for the admission not of unturbulent people but of men and women, in his words, "who see the ministry more as a mission than [as] a haven."[12] It remains a fact of contemporary seminary existence in North America that too many of our students (and faculty) demand of the theological institution that it *be* the cave, and remain bitterly and vocally critical of it when and as it declines so to function.

For all the legitimacy of the cave *trip*, the Word that comes when we emerge from the cave where alone the Word is accessible to us— the Word that comes is always the same: "What are you doing here? Do you know what you are doing here? And, if you know why you have come, then go back to what and where and who you were."

Paulo Freire says that we "are not built in silence, but in word, in work, in action-reflection." And in a note on that statement he comments:

I obviously do not refer to the silence of profound meditation [could we say, the cave], in which [one] only apparently leaves the world, withdrawing from it in order to consider it in its totality, and thus remaining with it. But this type of retreat is only authentic when the meditator is "bathed" in reality; not when the retreat signifies . . . flight from [the world], in a type of "historical schizophrenia."[13]

At a 1974 meeting of the Central Committee of the World Council of Churches in West Berlin the chairman, Dr. M. M. Thomas, said almost wistfully, at the conclusion of an address insisting (these were not his terms) on the inseparability of the Word of God and the word of earth: "I sometimes wish . . . that we could interpret [the theme] 'Christ only' as withdrawal from these many worlds and many responsibilities. But we cannot, because in and through Christ God renews all [persons] and all things."

In the same address he had earlier said:

As both a temporal and spiritual being, [one cannot] be involved in a purely "horizontal" or purely "vertical" activity; the horizontal/vertical, the social/spiritual dimensions meet in human nature and in all human aspirations and activities. . . . Living theology is a dialogue between the gospel of Christ and the self-understanding of men and women in concrete situations. . . . [So] evangelistic witness must be related to the deepest concerns of men and women.[14]

"What are you doing here, Elijah?" You may stay overnight, as it were, in the cave; but you may not *stay* in the cave, shut off from the word of earth, and so from Word of God. This is the very Word of God: Go back now, to hear and heed the word of earth!

Do we understand in church and seminary what Freire is talking about when he says that people "*cannot* save themselves (no matter how one understands 'salvation'), either as individuals or as an oppressor class. Salvation can be achieved only *with* others."? [15]

And it is Rosemary Ruether who suggests that there are two ways falsely to appropriate the transcendent. One is to domesticate it; the other is to separate it, isolate the Word, cut it away from the whole of human life. "Both the establishment [domestication] of Christianity and the segregation of the sacred to a sphere removed from the midst of life are equally ways of abolishing the presence of the Holy Spirit, so that the world of the powers and principalities can go on as before." [16]

Domestication is the double altar. It is Baalism. The attempt at sustained separation is cavism, tolerable, acceptable, even therapeutic as temporary expedient, but quickly self-defeating since word of earth and, in consequence, Word of God are shut away.

"What are you doing here, Elijah? ... Go back the way you have come; because there are still *seven thousand* [thousands upon thousands, a multitude, vast throngs] ... whose knees have never bent to Baal, nor whose lips have kissed him!"

THE WAY BACK FROM THE CAVE: VV. 19-21

It is possible, as an occasional textual critic has suggested, and as *The Jerusalem Bible* footnotes, that the closing verses of 1 Kings 19 are transferred or borrowed from the Elisha cycle of stories. Be that as it may, these lines offer a sharply appropriate climax to the narrative of the Cave.

(Vv. 19-21) *Leaving that place....*
Leaving the cave....
[Elijah] came upon Elisha son of Shaphat plowing with twelve yoke of oxen in front of him, and he with the twelfth. As Elijah passed by, he tossed his robe over him. Leaving the oxen ...

The Hebrew term may be stronger than this. "Leaving" suggests that Elisha may momentarily return. But the verb probably connotes the act of forswearing, of abandonment of all that is represented in *habaqar* the oxen or, better, the cattle, as the symbol of the life and work from which now Elisha means to separate himself, permanently and with finality. His very brief return, in a moment, is a ritual performance of that intention.

Leaving the oxen, [Elisha] ran after Elijah and said, "Let me give my father and mother a farewell kiss; then I will follow you." Elijah said to him, "Go on back: what claim have I got over you?" Leaving him, Elisha went back, took the pair of oxen, slaughtered them, used the implements [of plowing] to cook their flesh, and gave [it] to the people to eat. Then he left to follow Elijah, and he became his disciple.

Don't misunderstand me; which may only be a way of saying to myself, Don't let me misunderstand me. The cave may be good, recreative, restorative, and therefore essential; but not cavism, which would institutionalize the cave. Cave, *si*; cavism, *no!* The cave gives shelter when the furies without and within are raging beyond all control, and the Word comes more easily and distinctly after the grateful sound of gentle silence and our emergence from this place of isolation and security. It is now that we know, in the Word of God and the word of earth, that we are not alone, that we are surrounded in fact by clouds of living witnesses, that there is the work of the kingdom to be done, and disciples and colleagues, intimate Elishas, with whom to be doing the work.

Go back. Always go back; and on the way, always on the way, find, commission, enlist, and inspire Elisha and Elisha and Elisha. Go—with the Word of God and the word of earth.

Go, with Elijah and Elisha. Go, with Gustavo Gutierrez, who would bid us be mindful of that great company of anonymous Christians who, unable for compelling reasons to name the name of Yahweh/Christ, are nevertheless among the thousands who have not and will not bow down to Baal; and who reminds us that, in Christ, God has "irreversibly committed himself to the present moment of mankind [he means, of course, every present moment] to carry it to its fulfillment."[17]

Go with Elijah and Elisha.

Go with Dom Helder Camara, who, on rare and intimate terms with the bitter word of Brazilian earth as well as with the Word of God, is nevertheless able to declare:

I believe in a Creator and Father, who desired man [and woman] as co-Creators and who gave [them] intelligence and a creative imagination to dominate the universe and to complete the Creation . . . and he constantly sends his Spirit to make the human mind fruitful, even as he made the waters fertile at the beginning of Creation.[18]

Go with Elijah and Elisha—and with Paulo Freire, who, against odds much greater than we see or know, affirms his trust, as he says simply, "in the people," and his faith "in the creation of a world in which it will be easier to love."[19]

Go with Rainer Maria Rilke, too, who on August 12, 1904 wrote from Sweden to a young poet he never met (what a good Elijah person he was!):

We must assume our existence as broadly as we in any way can; everything, even the unheard of, must be possible in it. That is at bottom the only courage that is demanded of us: to have courage for the most strange, the most singular and the most inexplicable that we may encounter. That mankind has in this sense been cowardly has done life endless harm; the experiences that are called "vision," the whole so-called "spirit-world," death, all those things that are so closely akin to us, have by daily parrying been so crowded out of life that the senses with which we could have grasped them are atrophied. To say nothing of God.[20]

In the same letter he writes, "We have no reason to mistrust our world, for it is not against us [Rilke too has heard the rebuke at the mouth of the Cave]. If it has terrors, they are our terrors; if it has abysses, those abysses belong to us; [and] if there are dangers at hand, we must try to love them."[21]

Go with Elijah and Elisha. Go with all these. Go even with Gary MacEoin's conscientized Latin-American priests who choose to stay within the church and who do not, he writes, "see themselves as conduits of grace to tens of thousands of people. They are satisfied if they can create a few small islands of Christian life, leaving the future radiation to the Holy Spirit."[22]

We will go to the cave as we may and must when the time and place of our present moment become unendurable, when, in whatever way, we hear the terrifying word of threatened, unqualified disaster: If you are Elijah, I am Jezebel! But we will take only temporary lodging there. We will resist the drift or the drive toward cavism in ourselves, in the church and in seminary, and in the life of faith. On our way, always on our way in the earth, we will bring Elisha with us to the work of the Word of God and the word of earth;

if we cannot do more—it is enough—we will create islands of authentic Christian life, and we will be content in faith to leave the future radiation to the Holy Spirit.

IV
THE INHERITANCE:
1 KINGS 21

1   Now it happened that one Naboth of Jezreel owned a vineyard
2   adjacent to Ahab's [winter] residence; until one day Ahab
made this offer to Naboth: "Let me have your vineyard to use
as a vegetable garden, since it immediately adjoins my property. In exchange, I will give you a better vineyard, or, if you
3   prefer, I will pay you its worth in cash." But Naboth replied to
Ahab, "Yahweh forbid that I should give you my ancestral
inheritance!"

4   So Ahab returned home sullen and seething over Naboth's
refusal to relinquish his ancestral inheritance. He lay down on
his bed, averted his face, and refused to eat anything.

5   But then his wife, Jezebel, came to him and said, "What has
6   you so upset that you won't [even] eat anything?" So he told
her, "I made a proposal to Naboth. I said to him, 'Give me your
vineyard for cash or, if you prefer, I will give you a vineyard in
exchange for it.' But he said, 'I will not give you my vineyard.'"
7   His wife, Jezebel, answered him, "Do you or do you not
exercise rule over Israel? Snap out of it, eat something, and
take heart! I will myself present you with Naboth's vineyard!"

8   Accordingly, she wrote letters in Ahab's name, sealing them
with his seal; and she sent the letters to the elders and freemen
9   who were Naboth's fellow council members. This was the
message: "Proclaim a fast, with Naboth presiding over the
11, 12 convocation." They did as Jezebel told them to do: they pro-
13   claimed a fast and set Naboth over the assembly. But now two
men sitting near him testified against Naboth before the people
with the charge, "Naboth cursed God and king!" So they took
him out of town and stoned him to death.

14   The message was sent to Jezebel that Naboth had been stoned
15   and was dead; and as soon as Jezebel received it, she said to
Ahab, "Go ahead now; take possession of Naboth's vineyard
which he refused to give you for [hard] cash. For Naboth no
16   longer lives: he is dead!" Immediately at the word of Naboth's
death, Ahab started on his way to take possession of Naboth's
vineyard.

17, 18 But the Word of Yahweh occurred, and spoke to Elijah: "Be on
your way now to confront Ahab king of Israel; you will find

19 him in Naboth's vineyard where he has gone to take possession of it. You will give him this message: "Thus says Yahweh: Having murdered, do you even now take possession? In the place where the dogs licked Naboth's blood they shall lick your blood!"

20 Ahab said to Elijah, "Have you found me, O my enemy?" Elijah replied, "I have found you."

A RILKE WORD

Some years ago a seminary student in one of my classes wrote in a paper on the Call of Isaiah:

Would that the terms of my own call were so plain and pronounced. It would seem that one could hardly be half-hearted or uncertain about one's mission if one were given marching orders against a backdrop of tremors and smoke and seraphic adoration. I'd say that Isaiah got a good deal.

All of us who know, however underwhelmingly, the call to prophetic leadership, lay or ordained, are very well aware of what this seminarian is talking about; and in this sense there is, I am afraid, something almost inescapably deceiving in the stance of the preacher/lecturer/writer—at least this one. In his *Letters to a Young Poet,* Rilke at least twice insists on his own inadequacy or vulnerability, and in some appropriate way I would like to claim the sense of his demurrers. In the beginning of the second letter, explaining that he is still recovering from an illness, he says that "writing comes hard to me, and so you must take these few lines for more."[1] My own lines in these essays may not have been few enough; but they have not come easy, and I pray that by your own appropriation of them, and by the power of the Holy Spirit brooding always among us, you may receive them as more than given.

Rilke's eighth letter concludes, "Do not believe that he who seeks to comfort you lives untroubled. . . . His life has much difficulty and sadness and remains far behind yours. Were it otherwise he would never have been able to find these words."[2] This is not to say that it has been my intention only to comfort you, but rather that if and when I may have spoken in such a way as to appear to be without doubt and frustration and anguish, it has to do again with the stance that the occasion of lecturing/writing thrusts upon me. All of which is in part by way of saying thank you for the hearing/reading you have given me.

WORD OF GOD, WORD OF EARTH

These are not times in which comfort is easily come by; or, if it is, it may be insubstantial, or bought in a corrupt transaction of exchange of Word of God and word of earth for the obsessive word of the trivial, encapsulated world in which one is oneself the undisputed center. Take, for example, the case of the successful young man writing in *Guideposts* from his home in Palm Beach, Florida, in a feature called A Spiritual Workshop and titled, "How to Begin a Glorious Day."[3] I quote this in disapproval not so much of what is said, but of what is not said. This piece is one-dimensional, parochial. It belongs with other expressions of essential privatism.

I open my eyes. It is 5 A.M. I slide from the bed to my knees and pray before quickly slipping on some shorts, a sweat shirt, socks and jogging shoes. It's still dark outside when I open the front door. A warm breeze is blowing in from the ocean.

Soon I am jogging along Route A-1-A, beside the ocean. . . . As I jog along, I begin my spiritual exercise.

"Thank You, Lord, for this day. . . . " I thank Him for strong legs and a healthy body. In prayer, I review all my blessings.

My prayer turns to people. *Loved ones, friends, business contacts.* I name them out loud, those near and far. And then our leaders. "Lord, give them courage to take a stand for You."

The miles tick off. Two golden shafts come strong out of the sea and fade away into the morning sky. They remind me of a giant ladder which leads up to the heavens. Jacob dreamed of a ladder which went to Heaven and there at the top was the Lord, who told Jacob, "I am with thee." I meditate on that.

"Be with *me*, Lord," I pray. . . .

An orange ball appears at the rim of the ocean. The two golden poles of the ladder split into multi-colored shafts of light. The vast panorama across the eastern sky is changing.

I am back home now, refreshed and strengthened for a glorious new day.*

This is an experience of earth, to be sure—ocean, beach, the spectacular light of the sun as refracted through the earth's atmosphere, and the feet of the young jogger beating strongly, steadily, against the face of the ground. But it is an experience which has little if anything to do with the word of earth; it is an exercise which may in fact be calculated to shut out, to shut away, the real word of earth. And if it is an experience of God, it is god with a small "g," an idolatrous experience, self-aggrandizing, titillating, not far removed from the sensuousness of Baalism, over against which Elijah stands.

*Reprinted by permission from *Guideposts Magazine,* Copyright 1974 by Guideposts Associates, Inc., Carmel, New York 10512.

In any case, how far removed is this self-contented jogger from the authentic apprehension of Word of God and word of earth. Dom Helder Camara, the diminutive Brazilian archbishop who symbolizes Christian opposition to military dictatorship not only in Brazil but throughout Latin America, was awarded an honorary doctorate of laws at Harvard University in 1974. The citation might have read, "For rare and courageous sensitivity and commitment to Word of God and word of earth." It read, in fact, "The most Reverend Helder Camara, Doctor of Laws. A tireless opponent of poverty and injustice, a stalwart Christian leader offering life and hope to the downtrodden and defeated."[4]

It was an event ignored, of course, in Brazil. And even Harvard gave him no chance to deliver the speech he had prepared for the occasion. But *Harvard Magazine* reported it, and *Christianity and Crisis* printed it.[5] His words point out the utter vacuity of the jogger's "religious" intoxication.

He said the pessimist in him mocked his receipt of a degree in law when "law is ever more a hollow word, resonant but empty, in a world increasingly dominated by force, by violence, by fraud, by injustice, by avarice—in a word, by egoism"; when civil law permits "the progressive and rapid increase of oppressed people who continue being swept toward ghettos, without work, without health, without instruction, without diversion and, not rarely, without God"; when under so-called international law "more than two-thirds of humanity [exist] in situations of misery, of hunger, of subhuman life"; and when agrarian law or spatial law permits "today's powerful landowners to continue to live at the cost of misery for unhappy pariahs"; and whereby "modern technology achieves marvels from the earth with an ever-reduced number of rural workers [while] those not needed in the fields live sublives in depressing slums on the outskirts of nearly all the large cities."

Dom Helder speaks of "subwork leading to sublife . . . of the greed of multinationals that export entire factories to paradises of investment where salaries are low and dispute impossible . . . [of] dictatorships of the right or left but also pseudodemocracies turned shortsighted by obsessions such as anti-communism."

Dom Helder Camara: word of earth.

The speech ends on the note of the Word of God in response to the word of earth:

The degree with which you honor me brings me to ask of God that at this point of life . . . I spend myself to the end in the service of humankind—as the most secure means of giving glory to our Lord.

God permit that the symbol of my life be a candle that burns itself, that consumes itself while there is still wax to burn; when nothing more remains to be consumed, that my flame, yet an instant, dare to remain alive and afoot, to rumble after, happy in the conviction that one day the force of Right will conquer the pretended right of force.

Word of God, word of earth!

ON ADJACENCY

This Jezreel event[6] of coveted adjacent property and of subsequent treachery and murder for the sake of possession—this particular crisis of adjacency happened in the middle of the ninth century before our era, well over twenty-eight hundred years ago. With variation, but in essential correspondence of members of the plot, it happened of course throughout the spreading human family in the centuries and years, perhaps even months or days, preceding; and it has most assuredly continued to happen, in its significant essence, with persistence and always accompanying human carnage down to our own time and decade and, who knows, even day and hour. It may be happening even among us today or yesterday or tomorrow, on a simpler scale, of course, with covetousness, treachery, murder, and possession all symbolized in aggression against the psyche of another, an adjacent person. The resultant human carnage in such a case takes the form of a sophisticated psychological increment to a sustained, subtle process of essential dehumanization of a spouse or colleague or anyone in the array of personal relationships.

The recurrent phenomenon may be described as the problem of adjacency. Let us call the two parties A and B. B's property or treasure, B's heritage, B's right, is adjacent, or appears to be adjacent, or is declared to be adjacent—adjacency is a phenomenally flexible term, subject to interpretation according to what is deemed to be adjacent by the powerful covetor; B's thing which is B's by rights, by inheritance, becomes in its adjacency an object of passionate desire, an obsessive craving, on the part of a more powerful A. In the classical expression of the problem of adjacency, of which the story before us is a splendid example, the ensuing conflict of interest between A and B proves to be irreconcilable, and the weaker B is effectively eliminated as a contender. This is done, in this remarkable human family of which we are all a part, with demonic craft by the powerful, in an absolutely dazzling array of forms (if necessity is the mother of invention, covetousness and lust are the parents of ingenuity), upon well-established but shamelessly fraudulent justification, usually in the broad sense religious and sometimes even specifically theological. The more heinous the perpetuation of violence issuing from the problem of adjacency, the more probable, not to say imperative, the establishment of grounds in essential piety. This is to ensure the crucial support ostensibly of God himself (one suspects A always knows better), but, failing that, at least the consent of the rank and file of God's would-be worshipers.

In practice, of course, problems of adjacency are often resolved by the capitulation of B. I cannot speak for you, but if I had been in Naboth's place I think I would certainly have been tempted to say, What is this inheritance of mine or what do I care about my right when looked at over against what my refusal may cost me, or what I may gain by currying favor with the powerful A, and by striking with him an advantageous deal into the bargain? But this is not Naboth. Allende of Chile may well have been a Naboth. He refused to sell his inheritance and died at the sure instigation of a coalition of Ahabs—some of them having the initials CIA. History may well adjudge Castro of Cuba to be a Naboth who survived a US/Ahab plot to murder and take possession. Jezebel's Bay of Pigs was successful when ours was not. And Dom Helder Camara, who stands as both a Naboth and an Elijah on behalf of all victims of covetousness and appropriation, may, following some of his associates, suffer Naboth's elimination—God forbid! If it happens, it will of course be claimed that Dom Helder too had cursed God and the ruling military junta.

Olive Schreiner, an Englishwoman of South Africa, born in the middle of the nineteenth century and surviving well into the twentieth, was in many perceptive ways vastly ahead of her time. Of the sensitive English persons of her own place and generation she wrote, "We know, none so well, how stained is our African record; we know with what envious eyes the Government of English Ahabs eyes the patrimony of Black Naboths and takes it, if necessary, after bearing false witness against Naboth."[7] The government of US Ahabs has followed and outstripped the English lead. Like the claim of the old British Empire, we too can say that the sun never sets on fields and lands, on kingdoms and governments, on men and women and children, on myriads of Naboths—all adjacent to us. We play the grim game of adjacency with our own oppressed minorities and, as well, whether with Naboth's capitulation or elimination, with populations from Santiago to Saigon, from San Juan to Seoul. It is a tragedy of as yet unmeasured consequence that all over Latin America Nelson Rockefeller symbolizes the US Ahab; and we have reason to wonder whether the present administration may not be contemplating playing Ahab to the Naboth of the oil countries. In fact, of course, Naboth's vineyard, adjacent to US property, is a global phenomenon, and in devious ways we twist the circumstances to fit the charge, or misinterpret the charge to justify murder and possession—"Naboth cursed God and the king!"

I do not mean to say that our ruthless invocation of adjacency is anything new. Born and brought up in China, I believed then that China was ours. It was a long two weeks by ship from North America, but at least in spirit and in potential, it was adjacent, and we rather claimed it as our own vineyard. I do not repudiate my parents' work in China—largely in education—in quoting this passage from David Halberstam's *The Best and the Brightest:*

To America [in quoting that term for the United States, I apologize to all other Americans from Canada to Southern Chile and Argentina for this unwarranted appropriation] China was a special country, different from other countries. India could have fallen [he is referring to the collapse of Chiang Kai-shek in 1949], or an African nation, and the reaction would not have been the same. For the American missionaries loved China; it was, by and large, more exciting than Peoria [so that Peoria does not have to stand alone, let me say that my father certainly found Shanghai more exciting seventy years ago than Auburn, Alabama], had a better life style and did not lack for worthy pagans to be converted; add to that the special quality of China, a great culture, great food, great charm, and the special relationship was cemented. The Chinese were puritanical, clean, hard-working, reverent, cheerful, all the virtues Americans most admired. And so a myth had grown up, a myth not necessarily supported by the facts, of the very special U.S.-China relationship. We helped them and led them, and in turn they loved us. A myth fed by millions of pennies put in thousands of church plates by little children to support the missionaries in their work in this exotic land which was lusting for Christianity. China was good; the Chinese were very different from us, and yet they were like us;

what could be at once more romantic, yet safer. The Japanese were bad, more suspicious and could not be trusted. The Chinese were good and could be trusted.[8]

In 1950 Joseph Alsop wrote a three-part series entitled "Why We Lost China." Halberstam comments that "it was not a serious bit of journalism, but rather a re-creation of the Chennault-Chiang line. It set the tone . . . for the conspiracy view of the fall of China. . . . The title is worth remembering: 'Why We Lost China.' China was ours, and it was something to lose . . . countries were ours, we could lose them."[9]

And since the adjacent vineyard of China was not, after all, for barter, the US Ahab withdrew, sullen and seething, with face steadfastly averted for more than two decades. It remains to be seen what kind of plot, in detail, we shall resort to in hope of achieving some kind of resurrection of that once beneficent and lucrative relationship. It is already clear that that plot will involve the purchase and planting of false witnesses and the old charge that God and king, religion and democratic order, have been cursed.

We know, none so well, how stained is our national record; we know with what envious eyes our own business and military and political Ahabs regard the inheritance of Third World Naboths and take it, if necessary after bearing false witness against Naboth.

BY VIOLATION AND VIOLENCE

Elijah's successor prophets in the next century decry the lust for adjacent land; and they do so, of course, among a people in whose corporate understanding inherited property is a part of one's "psychological totality."[10] Several decades ago, Johannes Pedersen called attention to

the terror ringing through [Naboth's] answer to the proposal of the king. . . . Naboth cannot part with the property which he has inherited from his [ancestors] without committing sacrilege against himself and his kindred, so closely do kindred and property belong together. . . . In all the laws of the Old Testament it is taken absolutely for granted that no one sells . . . landed property without being forced to do so.[11]

It is this sense of the identity of person and property that intensifies Isaiah's denunciation of those "who join house to house, who add field to field [5:8]." And whether the juxtaposition is editorial or not, this cry of woe follows immediately upon the concluding verse of the Song of the Vineyard (5:1-7, RSV):

> The vineyard of the Lord of hosts is the house of Israel,
> and the [people] of Judah are his pleasant planting;
> and he looked for justice, but behold, bloodshed;
> for righteousness, but behold, a cry!

Micah's indictment is characteristically even more passionate (and one almost wonders whether both prophets explode as they do impelled, even if unconsciously, by the then already classical model of the Naboth incident). *The New English Bible* puts it this way (Micah 2:1-2):

> Shame on those [the old "woe" form] who lie in bed planning
> evil and wicked deeds
>   and rise at daybreak to do them,
>   knowing that they have the power!
> They covet land and take it by force;
>   if they want a house they seize it;
> they rob one of one's home
>   and steal every one's inheritance.

It was Jezebel who planned and executed the evil by which not only Naboth's inheritance but his very life was taken. To the brooding king she says, this product of the religion of Baal, devoid of Yahwism's sense of justice and righteousness, "Do you or do you not exercise rule over Israel!" There is an insinuation of incredulity laced with disdain and scorn. The German Roman Catholic scholar A. Šanda admirably paraphrases, *"Du bist mir ein feiner König!"* "A fine king you are for me!" [12] Knowing that we Ahabs and Jezebels have the power, and wanting Naboth's land and inheritance, we will take it by force of violence; but we will see to it that our punishment of Naboth fits his "crime" against us. As he in the name of Yahweh refused us the acquisition of vineyard, so we, in the name of that same Yahweh, will do away with Naboth and seize his inheritance. [13]

IN THE NAME OF GOD
It is, alas, all too devastating a parable of our own times and kingdoms; of our own pentagons, war departments, international peddlers of arms; of our own multinational corporations; of our own

and allied governments. In the primary if not sole interest of maintaining and enhancing what we possess—in this world in truth like a royal residence and grounds in Jezreel—we plan our evil deeds and rise at daybreak to do them, knowing that we have the power; and what we covet we will take, be it even another's inheritance of life, of dignity, of humanity. We will appropriate what is Naboth's to have and to hold from this day forward, for better, for worse, to love and to cherish, till death us do part—and we will do it ostensibly *according to God's holy ordinance.* We take it where we will and can, from our own minority Naboths to the Naboths in the Caribbean, in Central and South America, and on the continents of Africa and Asia. We do what we do in the way of appropriation and, if need be, murder with all the craft of a Jezebel. We do it, by cunning, by power and prestige, by elaborately contrived false witness—we too do it claiming the while that it is done in the name of Yahweh, according to God's holy ordinance, even in the name of Jesus Christ, and of course because we are a Christian nation. You know: In God We Trust. And so, wherever we do it, we insist that we do it for you, you who survive our doing it. We do it to make your world safe for democracy (our brand of democracy, of course). We steal or destroy your inheritance to protect you from Godless communism (which of course also threatens our own power and wealth). We do it to help you build airports and highways for your use, of course (but also so that we may the more easily exercise our prerogatives of adjacency).

And dearly beloved, I do not know how or whether we shall stop it until it is too late, even for us.

The "we" that I've been using—the first-person pronoun plural— deserves a word. Of course it is not you and I who are the instrumental perpetrators of covetous adjacency with its attendant treachery, murder, and seizure. It is not we who in any direct sense perform the act of the theft of the inheritance. I suspect that we are by and large among those whom our contemporaries on the far right call bleeding hearts, and they do emphatically mean that term pejoratively. They would also say of us, the bleeding hearts, that we—to exchange one metaphor for another—shed only crocodile tears. We would respond, most of us, that we do in fact bleed, that we know both outrage and anguish for what, for example, our treachery (on two fronts) and our arrogant power inflicted and continue to inflict on the lands and people of Cambodia and Vietnam; or, still a lot of us, for what we see as our unconscionable role in the overthrow of Allende. ITT and other previously thwarted covetors of Naboth's vineyard in Chile are right now reaping the fruits of murder by taking economic possession again.

Despite the tendency of the Elijah narratives to disparage Ahab, the facts about him clearly return the impression of a man and monarch of exceptional stature. 1 Kings 20 and 22 see him in rather better light than 17—19, 21. Except as viewed exclusively from the perspective of Yahwist fundamentalists or fanatics, he was a person of outstanding ability, integrity, and courage. He of course desperately wanted Naboth's inheritance. He was persuaded that he needed it. He no doubt convinced himself that he deserved it, that it was somehow his right, even as advertisers, from McDonalds to airline companies, seek to convince us that we *deserve* a break which is their product or service. And however acquired, he hoped that once possessed the whole matter of the vineyard could be forgotten.

Jezebel goes to work and Ahab stands by, as too often too many of us do. But in this democracy of ours, pseudo or real, the arrangements for the act of possession and the essential steps of pious subterfuge, false witness, indictment without defense, and finally violence and murder—all this is, in a manner of speaking, done in our name and sealed with our seal. It is done by leaders whom we elect (Gerald Ford and Nelson Rockefeller being marked recent exceptions), with the expenditure of our tax dollars, and, often with careful particularity, in alleged and ostensible concern for values purporting to be cherished among us in the religious establishment.

It is my simple and direct submission that in common practice in organized religion in the United States we have let our Jezebels set the stage for the effective dispossession of the inheritance of land, resources, productivity, and human dignity of weaker neighbors declared to be adjacent to us all around the globe. The vast majority of us in the church are able to live like relative Ahabs because Jezebel is scheming schemes and working works around the clock—in our name and, as it works out, also to our profit. And we do not want to look too closely; we cannot bring ourselves to renounce the ways of Jezebel even when we know that Naboth's vineyard is ours by treachery, violence, and murder. But woe are we, dearly beloved, we are undone, we are lost, if the church is silent, if no powerful, corporate, prophetic protest is made when in this Jezreel palace of ours there is violence instead of justice, a vast cry (increasingly bitter and militant) from the world's dispossessed instead of righteousness, and the practice of the right of force instead of the force of right.

THE QUESTION AND THE QUESTIONS

Was it really Jezebel who did it? Ahab knew, Ahab knew. Ahab always knows. *Jezebel wrote letters in Ahab's name, sealing them with his seal.* We know, we know. And Ahab always receives the word that Naboth's inheritance is his for the taking with grotesquely mingled feelings of satisfaction and dread. *Jezebel said to Ahab, "Go ahead now; take possession of Naboth's vineyard which he refused to give you for cash. For Naboth no longer lives: he is dead!"* Naboth is dispossessed. His inheritance is yours.

What is the word of earth? This is the word of earth—that Naboth is legion; that Naboth's essential inheritance, land, work, creativity, human dignity, is daily seized by the strong—and that we are among the strongest of the strong!

But the Word of God occurred, and spoke to Elijah: *"Be on your way now to confront Ahab king of Israel; you will find him in Naboth's vineyard where he has gone to take possession of it. You will give him this message: "Thus says Yahweh: Having murdered, do you even now take possession? In the place where the dogs licked Naboth's blood they shall lick your blood!"*

Question: To whom are we, church people of the United States, to whom are we preponderantly more analogous, Elijah or Ahab?

Question: Which is the more influential altar among us, that of Yahweh or of Baal, God or mammon, Christ or possessions?

Question: Is it not true that as a people we have in our whole history repeatedly and down to this present day murdered, in body but also spirit and psyche, in order to possess?

Question: Is it not true that by and large we of the church have been in consent, if not always with our ballots, then by our silence.

Question: Whose inheritance now sustains the life of relative wealth and plenty that is ours, our own (which we've spent and overspent) or that of a plurality of Naboths?

Question: Can we yet turn back the judgment that we too will die in our own blood where and because we have shed the innocent blood and seized the cherished human heritage of myriad, uncountable, unsung, powerless, and dispossessed Naboths—red, black, brown, yellow, and white?

Question: Can we revive and recreate Elijah among us; can the church, and we of the church, be prophet as well as priest to king and nation and world?

Ahab said to Elijah, "Have you found me, O my enemy?"
Elijah replied, "I have found you."

Georg Fohrer best returns the sense of it:

"Hast du mich gefunden?"—hast du mich endlich bei einem Verbrechen ertappt?
Und Elia antwortet: "Ich habe dich ertappt!"

And as Fohrer adds, *"Mit diesem Höhepunkt schloss die alte Erzählung."*[14]

The original narrative closed with this dramatic exchange. Ahab knew, he knew. He knew all along it wouldn't wash with Yahweh. We Ahabs always know; but there will be no confession, no turning, no cessation of the ways of Jezebel, no restitution, no redemption of the vast, total human inheritance except by the happening of the Word, its speaking again to Elijah, us, and Elijah's ministry, ours, to Ahab and Jezebel and the hordes of the always oncoming Naboths.

Have you (Fohrer's sense) at last caught me in the very act, O my enemy, my old enemy, my old friend, my old dreaded and cherished prophet; after all this, have you really uncovered me; after drought, after that contest of altars on Mount Carmel, after your flight from us in terror that took you all the way to your cave on Horeb—after all this have you caught me, exposed me, apprehended me by the Word of Yahweh, judged me in that same Word—and so, perhaps, in spite of judgment, opened the only possible way to my redemption? Have you found me, O my enemy—O Word of God, O Word of God incarnate?

And so the literal reading is best after all: I have found you. I think Ahab knew. Question: Do we? For it is only in being fully found by the Word of God that we may be saved, that we may hear and understand and heed the anguished, bitter, raucous, critical word of earth, and that the inheritance of us all may be preserved and enhanced to the glory of God and to the service of God's children of the earth.

APPENDIX: A STUDY GUIDE

BY TERUO KAWATA
ASSOCIATE SECRETARY
OFFICE FOR CHURCH LIFE AND LEADERSHIP
OF THE UNITED CHURCH OF CHRIST

CHAPTER I: THE DROUGHT

1. Circle the phrase which comes closest to summarizing the presentation:

   A. Elijah is a model for contemporary ministers because he always trusted that God would care for him.

   B. The "Word of God" and the "word of earth" are the same.

   C. Contemporary ministry is work to be done "between" the reading of the Bible and the reading of the newspaper.

   D. The prophetic is the only valid ministry.

   E. The word of earth must never intrude on the Word of God.

   F. Ministry is to preach God's word.

2. Dr. Napier says the word of earth is crisis, i.e., that there is a new day of Third World claims, and that things are not going to be the same anymore; moreover, that the resources of the earth are being exhausted and that we are coming to a time of drought. How has this "word of earth" affected your life, and how do you feel about it?

3. There are three scenes in Chapter 17 of 1 Kings: Elijah being fed by the ravens, Elijah as the guest of the widow and her son, and the sickness of the son. What do these vignettes in Elijah's life say to the contemporary church about its ministry?

CHAPTER II: THE ALTARS

1. Circle the sentences that have to do with the crisis of the earth:

   A. We have vandalized the resources of the earth.

   B. The Communists are taking over nation after nation.

   C. The Third World peoples are causing trouble.

   D. The exploited of the earth are rising up with new claims.

   E. The old values are no longer upheld.

2. What did Elijah mean when he said to Ahab, "I'm not the one who's troubled Israel, but you"?

3. Who are the troublers of the earth today?

4. For Elijah, the issue was between two altars: worship of God and worship of Baal. What are the alternatives, or double altars, that claim our attention? (List on newsprint.)

5. Dr. Napier suggests that for Elijah to slaughter the prophets of Baal is a call to a radical separation and break between the two altars. What could such a radical break mean for our churches?

CHAPTER III: THE CAVE

1. Circle the statement that best summarizes the presentation:

   A. No minister should ever run away and hide from her/his critics.

   B. God will always take care of you, so you need not be afraid of anything.

   C. It is all right to go to the cave when things get too rough and frightening, so long as you don't stay there.

   D. The role of the church is to be a cave.

2. What are some of the Jezebel experiences in our time that threaten and frighten?

3. What are the caves in which the people of our time seek to escape?

4. In what ways are our churches caves?

5. Dr. Napier says, "For all the legitimacy of the cave trip, the word that comes when we emerge from the cave where alone the Word is accessible to us—the Word is always the same: "What are you doing here? Do you know what you are doing here? And, if you know why you have come, then go back to what and where and who you were." What does this say to you personally? To your church?

CHAPTER IV: THE INHERITANCE

1. Why did Naboth refuse to exchange or sell his property to Ahab?

2. What would be so precious to you that you would not let any Ahab take over?

3. Where in your experience or knowledge has Ahab moved in on Naboth? (List on newsprint.)

4. When might it be right for Ahab to move in on Naboth?

5. Is your church more like Ahab (who stood by while Jezebel murdered Naboth) or Elijah? List the ways in which it has acted like Ahab, the ways it has acted like Elijah.

6. What does Dr. Napier mean when he has Ahab say, "Have you at last caught me . . . O my enemy, my old enemy, my old friend, my old dreaded and cherished prophet; after all this, have you really uncovered me . . . exposed me, apprehended me by the Word of Yahweh, judged me in that same Word—and so, perhaps, in spite of judgment, opened the only possible way to my redemption"?

NOTES

PREFACE

1. Gerhard von Rad, *Old Testament Theology,* trans. D. M. G. Stalker (New York: Harper & Row, 1965), vol. II, p. 14. Cf. the somewhat differing view of Helmer Ringgren: "In large measure these narratives bear the stamp of legend, but they undoubtedly contain reliable historical reminiscences." *Israelite Religion,* trans. David E. Green (Philadelphia: Fortress Press, 1966), p. 261.

2. Von Rad, op. cit., p. 6: "It was in the ninth century, with Elijah and Elisha, that prophecy . . . first began to make its voice heard."

CHAPTER I: THE DROUGHT

1. Rubém Alves, *A Theology of Human Hope* (St. Meinrad, Ind.: Abbey Press, 1972), p. 71.

2. Quoted by Gustavo Gutierrez, *A Theology of Liberation*, trans. Sister Caridad Inda and John Eagleson (Maryknoll, N.Y.: Orbis Books, 1972), p. 12, from Congar, *Situation et tâches présentes de la théologie* (Paris: 1967), p. 72.

3. Quoted in Donella H. Meadows et al., *The Limits to Growth* (New York: Universe Books, 1972), p. 17.

4. Ibid., p. 44; quoted from "The Biosphere," *Scientific American*, September 1970, p. 53.

5. Ibid., pp. 23f.

6. Ibid., p. 24.

7. Cf. Amos 9:7 and Isaiah 19:23-25.

8. Numbers 20:10, NEB; cf. Exodus 17:1ff. and see Psalm 106:33.

9. Used by permission of John Fry.

10. Gutierrez, op. cit., pp. 7f., again quotes Congar (op. cit., p. 27): "Seen as a whole, the direction of theological thinking has been characterized by a transference away from attention to the being per se of supernatural realities, and toward attention to their relationship with man, with the world, and with the problems and the affirmations of all those who for us represent the Others."

11. See my article, "The Omrides of Jezreel," *Vetus Testamentum*, vol. 9 (1959), pp. 366-78. See also O. H. Steck, *Überlieferung und Zeitgeschichte in den Elia-Erzählungen* (Neukirchen-Vluyn: 1968), p. 57, note 4.

12. Luke 9:11-17, after RSV and NEB.

13. See preceding note 6 (*The Limits to Growth*, p. 24).

14. Numbers 11:11-15, NAB.

15. Job 7:17-19. The translation is that of Marvin H. Pope in *Job*, in the series *The Anchor Bible*, vol. 15, rev. ed. (Garden City, N.Y.: Doubleday, 1973), p. 58.

16. Jeremiah 20:7-9, RSV adapted.

17. Habakkuk 1:2-4, JB.

CHAPTER II: THE ALTARS

1. This is not translation but paraphrase. The reading I prefer of the four Hebrew words is: So that this people may know "that you turned their heart backward"; that is, that you, Yahweh, are responsible, not Baal, for the backward heart. The alternative literal reading of the Hebrew is in any case implicit; that is, "that it is you who brings them back" (to their authentic allegiance). The sense is not ambiguous. It is as Rashi put it (Rabbi Solomon bar Isaac, that magnificent rabbinic scholar of the eleventh century), "Thou gavest them place to depart from thee, and in thy hand it is to establish their heart toward thee." See further James A. Montgomery in Montgomery and Gehman, *The Book of Kings*, in the series *The International Critical Commentary* (New York: Charles Scribner's Sons, 1951), p. 305.

2. One cannot but wonder whether "Elijah" may not have been an assumed name, a name given to the prophet subsequent to the event underlying the present narrative (whatever its factual proportions). The name means "My God is Yahweh," or even simply "God is Yahweh."

3. "For [this] ugly sequel, if authentic, the history of religion and politics down to our own day is sad apology." So Montgomery, op. cit., p. 306. It appears to me to be in any case gratuitous to read, as Gunkel does (in an argument against the historicity of the event), "dass Elias die 450 Propheten Baals mit eigener Hand geschlachtet habe" (Hermann Gunkel, *Elias, Jahwe und Baal* [Tübingen: 1906], p. 36). The narrative does not here name the number, and it is improbable that all the prophets of Baal in the land were present at the Carmel assembly. The number 450 may not anywhere be reliable, and surely the statement that Elijah executed the Baal prophets does not require or warrant the reading "with his own hand."

4. This is, literally, the familiar biblical phrase "girded up his loins." NEB puts it nicely: "he tucked up his robe."

5. Charles Y. Glock et al., *Wayward Shepherds* (New York: Harper & Row, 1971), pp. 95 and 121f.

6. In a letter from *The Cousteau Society, Inc.*, Box 1716, Danbury, Connecticut 06816, July 1974, p. 1.

7. James B. Sterba, *The New York Times*, December 23, 1973; quoted in an undated letter from CROP, 919 North Emerald Avenue, Modesto, California 95351 (National Office: Box 968, Elkhart, Indiana 46514), on behalf of the Community Hunger Appeal of Church World Service.

8. Gustavo Gutierrez, *A Theology of Liberation* (Maryknoll, N.Y.: Orbis Books, 1972), pp. 26f.

9. Ibid., p. 88.

10. Gunkel, op. cit., p. 41.

11. Ibid., p. 48.

12. I have borrowed this phrase in this context from Montgomery, op. cit., p. 299: "The clash of words between (Ahab) and the undaunted man of God is classical. The epithet, *Troubler of Israel,* is flung back in the king's teeth."

13. In an address prepared for delivery at Harvard University, June 13, 1974, on the occasion of his receiving an honorary doctorate in recognition of his defense of human rights. The address appeared in *Christianity and Crisis,* vol. 34, no. 14, p. 176. The quotations that appear here are reprinted from that issue (August 5, 1974) of *Christianity and Crisis,* © copyright 1974 by Christianity and Crisis, Inc. Used by permission.

14. There is dispute over the antiquity and priority of the two altars on Carmel, and in particular concerning the status of the Yahweh altar. But the symbolism of the two altars is not in question.

15. Gerhard von Rad, *Old Testament Theology,* trans. D. M. G. Stalker (New York: Harper & Row, 1965), vol. II, p. 17. Von Rad further comments here on why the people do not answer Elijah. Their silence "argues lack of understanding of the question rather than any feeling of guilt (v. 21). Elijah had to make a Herculean effort before he succeeded in forcing them to make a decision for which no one saw the need."

16. James Cone tells us that in the black community this is known as "shuffling." *A Black Theology of Liberation* (Philadelphia: Lippincott, 1970), p. 122.

17. RSV, New York, 1952; JB, Garden City, N.Y., 1966; NAB, New York, 1971; NEB, New York, 1971.

18. James A. Montgomery, op. cit., p. 301.

19. J. Skinner, *Kings,* in the series *The Century Bible* (Edinburgh. Oxford University Press, 1904), p. 231.

20. Matthew 6:24; Luke 16:13.

21. Rosemary Radford Ruether, *Liberation Theology* (New York: Paulist-Newman, 1972), p. 176. Copyright © 1972 by The Missionary Society of St. Paul the Apostle in the State of New York. Used by permission of Paulist Press.

22. Montgomery, op. cit., p. 302.

23. As I have already commented (in note 3), it is quite unnecessary to insist that the text means to say that all 450 prophets in Israel (if that number is anywhere reliable) were present at the Carmel convocation and that Elijah himself, in person, was the executioner, dispatching them all *with his own hand.* So, again, Gunkel, op. cit., p. 36: "Wenn es heisst, dass Elias die 450 Propheten Baals mit eigener Hand geschlachtet habe, so finden wir dass ein wenig zu heldenhaft." This reading is certainly *de trop.*

24. Montgomery, op. cit., p. 306.

CHAPTER III: THE CAVE

1. E.g., Gerhard von Rad, *Old Testament Theology*, trans. D. M. G. Stalker (New York: Harper & Row, 1965), vol. II, p. 19.

2. Numbers 11:15.

3. Cf. Exodus 24:18 and 34:28, and Deuteronomy 9:9-11, 18 and 10:10.

4. Hosea 7:8. The term is uncommon, appearing only seven times in the Old Testament.

5. Cf. Exodus 19:18, 33:22, and 34:6.

6. Exodus 19:16, 18-19; 33:18-23, JB.

7. Of all these, and of all that these may represent, sex in love surely has the best claim. Rosemary Ruether in an essay on Judaism and Christianity tells us that "far from despising sexuality, the rabbis even declared that, since the destruction of the temple, the presence of God existed in two places: in the rabbinic houses of study, and when a man lies beside his wife." Ruether, *Liberation Theology* (New York: Paulist-Newman, 1972), p. 70. Copyright © 1972 by The Missionary Society of St. Paul the Apostle in the State of New York. Used by permission of Paulist Press.

8. *Webster's Third New International Dictionary* (Springfield: Merriam Company, 1965), italics mine.

9. Montgomery, *The Book of Kings* (New York: Charles Scribner's Sons, 1951), pp. 314f.

10. Skinner, *Isaiah, The International Critical Commentary*, p. 205.

11. See *Christianity and Crisis*, August 5, 1974, p. 177.

12. *The Continuing Quest*, ed. James B. Hofrenning (Minneapolis: Augsburg, 1970), p. 38.

13. Paulo Freire, *Pedagogy of the Oppressed*, trans. Myra Bergman Ramos (New York: Herder & Herder, 1970), p. 76, text and footnote.

14. See *This Month*, Ecumenical Press Service, World Council of Churches, Geneva, September 1974, pp. 4f.

15. Freire, op. cit., p. 142 (italics his).

16. Ruether, op. cit., p. 33.

17. Gutierrez, *A Theology of Liberation*, trans. Sister Caridad Inda and John Eagleson (Maryknoll, N.Y.: Orbis Books, 1972), pp. 71 and 76, and 15.

18. Camara, reprinted from the August 5, 1974 issue of *Christianity and Crisis*, p. 176. Copyright © 1974 by Christianity and Crisis, Inc. Used by permission.

19. Freire, op. cit., p. 24.

20. Rilke, *Letters to a Young Poet,* trans. M. D. Herter Norton (New York: W. W. Norton, 1954, 1962), p. 67.

21. Ibid., p. 69.

22. Gary MacEoin, *Revolution Next Door* (New York: Holt, Rinehart & Winston, 1971), p. 129.

CHAPTER IV: THE INHERITANCE

1. Rainer Maria Rilke, *Letters to a Young Poet*, trans. M. D. Herter Norton (New York: W. W. Norton, 1954, 1962), p. 23.

2. Ibid., p. 72.

3. *Guideposts*, Carmel, N. Y., August 1974, p. 19 (italics mine).

4. *Harvard Magazine*, vol. 76, no. 11 (July-August 1974), p. 63.

5. Reprinted from the August 5, 1974 issue of *Christianity and Crisis*, pp. 175-77. Copyright © 1974 by Christianity and Crisis, Inc. Used by permission. Richard J. Barnet and Ronald Müller, *Global Reach: The Power of the Multinational Corporations* (New York: Simon and Schuster, 1974), p. 184, give specific content to Dom Helder Camara's words: "Global companies have used their great levers of power—finance capital, technology, organizational skills, and mass communications—to create a Global Shopping Center in which the hungry of the world are invited to buy expensive snacks and a Global Factory in which there are fewer and fewer jobs. The World Manager's vision of One World turns out in fact to be two distinct worlds—one featuring rising affluence for a small transnational middle class, and the other escalating misery for the great bulk of the human family. The dictates of profits and the dictates of survival are in clear conflict."

6. My own reasons for seeing all the action as occurring in Jezreel are discussed in "The Omrides of Jezreel" in *Vetus Testamentum*, vol. 9 (1959), pp. 366-78.

7. Quoted in *A Track to the Water's Edge: The Olive Schreiner Reader*, ed. Howard Thurman (New York: Harper & Row, 1973), p. xxvii, from her *Thoughts on South Africa*, p. 345.

8. David Halberstam, *The Best and the Brightest* (New York: Random House, 1969), p. 143. Copyright © 1969, 1971, 1972 by David Halberstam. Used by permission of Random House, Inc.

9. Ibid., p. 144.

10. See Johannes Pedersen, *Israel: Its Life and Culture* (London: Oxford University Press, 1940), vol. I-II, p. 81.

11. Ibid., pp. 82f. Nevertheless, as H. Seebass has recently remarked in "Der Fall Naboth in 1 Reg. XXI," *Vetus Testamentum*, vol. 24 (1974), pp. 476f., there had to be conditions under which Naboth's vineyard was saleable or exchangeable, since otherwise Ahab's straightforward request and his response of bitter disappointment make no sense.

12. *Die Bücher der Könige*, 2 vols. (Münster: 1911); quoted in Montgomery and Gehman, *The Book of Kings* (New York: Charles Scribner's Sons, 1951), p. 331.

13. For this insight I am grateful to Seebass, op. cit., p. 481; "Von einem Urteil nirgendwo die Rede ist. Dagegen hatte Isebel die Genugtuung, dass Naboth (scheinbar zu Recht) *im Namen der Religion* gesteinigt wurde, wie er *im Namen der Religion* den Könige zurückgewiesen hatte" (italics his).

14. Georg Fohrer, *Elia*, vol. 53 in the series *Abhandlungen zur Theologie des Alten and Neuen Testaments* (Zürich, 2d ed., 1968), p. 28.

ABOUT THE AUTHOR

Davie Napier is President of Pacific School of Religion, Berkeley, California. Born in China, the son of missionary parents, he grew up in Nanking, Kobe, and Shanghai and is a graduate of Samford University, Yale Divinity School, and Yale University (Ph.D.). He has taught Old Testament and religion at Alfred University, University of Georgia, Yale University, and Stanford University. He has been Dean of the Chapel at Stanford University and prior to that was Master of Calhoun College of Yale University.

Dr. Napier is the author of numerous books including *From Faith to Faith, Song of the Vineyard, Prophets in Perspective, Come Sweet Death, On New Creation,* and *Time of Burning.* In 1975 he gave the Lyman Beecher Lectures at Yale Divinity School.